I0107779

Free to Flourish
Cultivating the Fruit of the Spirit

Unless otherwise noted, Scripture quotations are taken from the Holy Bible, New American Standard Version, Copyright 1994. PC Study Bible.
Verses marked NIV are taken from the New International Version, copyright 1994 PC Study Bible.

Free to Flourish: Cultivating the Fruit of the Spirit
Published by Motl Ministry Publications Copyright © 2006 by April Motl revised 2013 ALL RIGHTS RESERVED No part of this publication may be reproduced, stored in a retrieval system, or transmitted, in any form or by any means-electronic, mechanical, photocopying, recording or otherwise- without prior written permission.
To order additional copies, visit Motl Ministries www.MotlMinistries.com

Table Contents

. . . .

How Does Your Garden Grow?

· ·

Day One
A Life of Fruitfulness

Day Two
Good Soil

Day Three
Pulling Weeds

Day Four
Pest Control

Day Five
Taking Inventory

<u>*Key Verses:*</u>

You did not choose Me but I chose you, and appointed you that you would go and bear fruit, and that your fruit would remain, so that whatever you ask of the Father in My name He may give to you.

John 15:16

But the fruit of the Spirit is love, joy, peace, patience, kindness, goodness, faithfulness, gentleness, self-control; against such things there is no law. Galatians 5:22-23

Day One: A Life of Fruitfulness

There's a story about a little boy who went to the doctor's office. Once inside the examination room, the nurse checked his height, weight and heart. She could see he was a bit nervous. Believing that involving him in the process might calm his little boy nerves, she asked if he'd like to hear his heart with the stethoscope. When she placed the earpieces in his ears his expression changed to shock, surprise, and then delight. "Is that Jesus knocking on the door of my heart?" he exclaimed. The nurse, was surprised too. She'd never had anyone respond that way. She was a believer and told him "Yes, it is. You'd better make sure you answer Him!"

There are a whole lot of things knocking on the door of our hearts; and for many of us, there might be quite a lot banging around on the inside as well! For the sake of our study, imagine your heart as if it were a garden. What's growing in it? How's the quality of your soil? Are there places that need pruning, watering, or fertilizing? Are there bugs eating away at any of it?

Read over Galatians 5:16-24 and ask the Lord to illuminate your heart about the status of your "garden."

Write your reflections about the condition of the garden of your heart here. Is there one thing you'd like to see the Lord prune away or grow in you over the course of this study? Write a prayer to Him:

_____

_____

_____

_____

_____

_____

_____

_____

_____

_____

As a younger Christian I remember reading the fruit of the Spirit passage in Galatians 5:22-23. I wasn't able to say that my life was defined by those characteristics. At the same time, I didn't see my life as characterized by the fruit of the flesh either. I needed a spiritual Garmin or TomTom! I knew where I wanted to go, I just had NO clue how to get there!

Slowly the Lord showed me that the fruit of the Spirit and the fruit of the flesh traits weren't just a checklist to measure up against, or a set of on/off switches. They were more like destinations to head toward. It wasn't as if I were either one or the other; but rather, was I growing toward one or the other. I couldn't match up the traits to say I was either a loving girl or a witchcraft girl. Rather, the characteristics depicted two lifestyle destinations. For me, a main section of the path between where I was stuck and all that desired fruit of the Spirit, was a roadblock I couldn't see my way around. That "roadblock" was the healing of my emotions. I had runaway emotions that sucked the joy from my heart, robbed me of peace, quenched unconditional love, zapped my patience and self-control...oh, let's not even go there!

It was as if the garden of my heart had thick, heavy vines growing all over it in a tangled mess. I had no idea where to even begin to untangle my jungled mess. But God is faithful, even when, or perhaps especially when, we are in places where we can't help ourselves!

Identify one emotion in particular that you think might hinder your spiritual fruitfulness and journal your thoughts about your particular issue with that emotion.

_____

_____

_____

_____

I recently asked a woman how her grown children were doing. "Fruitful" she replied. She was referring to the number of grandchildren she was accumulating. You see, "fruitful" can refer to many different aspects of our lives. What does "fruitful" mean to you? When you die, will people say you lived a fruitful life? What are the ingredients of a fruitful life?

Read the following passages and journal the main idea(s) of each.

John 15:1-17

_____

_____

_____

_____

Ephesians 5:9-16

_____

_____

_____

Philippians 1:10-11

_____

_____

_____

Colossians 1:10-12

_____

_____

_____

Hebrews 13:15

_____

_____

_____

James 3:17-18

_____

_____

_____

Think over the garden of your heart and journal your responses to the following questions:

1. How has God pruned you? Did you bear more fruit after the experience?

_____

_____

_____

_____

2. Based on the passage from John 15, how is God glorified? Sometimes it is hard to discern the value of your service/obedience to the Lord, but have you seen Him grow fruit in your life recently? What was it?

_____

_____

_____

_____

3. Based on the Ephesians 5 passage, how might waking up spiritually be tied to your life producing more fruit? How have you perhaps fallen asleep morally or spiritually in a way that may have kept you from some of the fruitfulness God intended for you?

_____

_____

_____

_____

4. Based on the Philippians 1 passage, how do you think your personal purity is a factor in maintaining a fruitful life?

_____

_____

5. I love the Hebrews verse we read! Sometimes I have a too-big-mouth that gets me in trouble. How can we have lips that bear fruit to the Lord? How can you apply this to your life today?

_____

_____

_____

_____

6. Based on the verses from James, how are purity and peace tied to bearing fruit to the Lord?

_____

_____

_____

_____

7. From all these passages, what are you sowing into your life and legacy? What have you been reaping?

_____

_____

_____

_____

Spend some time in prayer committing the garden of your heart to the Lord. Rephrase Colossians 1:10-12 into a prayer.

_____

_____

_____

_____

Day Two: Good Soil

Yesterday we dug into the ideas behind fruitful living. I hope that God expanded your heart and mind to see a bigger vision of His heart for you in the area of fruitfulness. I pray you've had a renewed thirst to live in a way that would bear fruit for our Lord. Today we are going to study how the soil of our hearts affects our fruitfulness. So, let's dive into Matthew 13:3-23.

At different times in our life, the "seeds" God sends our way are met with different heart conditions. There was a time in my life when rebellion hardened the soil of my heart towards God's design for purity in my life. At other times, my heart has been wide open and soft towards the Lord; but birds and other pests stole away the seeds of truth.

Journal your thoughts for the following questions:

What condition is the soil of your heart in right now?

_____

_____

_____

What condition has it been in over the past year or so?

_____

_____

_____

Read the following verses and journal your heart response towards God's Word:

Hosea 6:3

_____

_____

Hosea 10:12

_____

_____

Isaiah 44:3-5

_____

_____

Isaiah 58:10-11

_____

_____

Isaiah 51:3

_____

_____

Isaiah 61:1-3

_____

_____

Jeremiah 17:7-10a

_____

_____

Some of the above verses reveal that our lives affect the way the Gardener waters, tends and cares for us. Others indicate that we can cry out to God and He will pour over us with cleansing, fresh water and make us flourish in Him.

Choose any of the verses from our study time today and use them to frame your own Scripture prayers asking for God to work in your heart. May you bask in the light of His love, revel in the cool, sheltering refreshment of His grace, and thrive in the truth of His Word - even if it means a little pruning or turning up of the soil in the garden of your heart!

_____

_____

_____

_____

Day Three: Weeds

For the purpose of this study, "weeds" are the things that crop up in our lives as a result of our natural, fleshly, human nature. In other words, "weeds" represent the sins in our lives.

Every time I have ever been in a study about the fruit of the Spirit, the teacher uses one of two approaches to the subject. The fruit was cultivated either by "working" at it or by praying for it. Since it is the work of God's Spirit within us, the "working" at it strategy seems unfruitful at best and untruthful at worst. But just praying for the fruit of the Spirit without knowing how to align my heart and life in obedience proved almost as unsuccessful in my experience as well. The reason being that God has certain principles about the way He generally conducts His work. Don't get me wrong - I'm not making up any spiritual laws about God. But there are principles as to how He works. Specifically, if I am holding on to sin in my life, He isn't as apt to grant me some particular spiritual blessing. My hands are full. If He were to place His gift in my hands, it would simply fall away because right now I have my hands full with my own sin. It isn't until my hands are empty that He generally chooses to fill them with His good things.

Scripture refers to a "quenching of the Spirit" and this is what I am talking about here. Our sin quenches the work of God in our lives. So no matter how much we pray for love, joy or peace, if we are hanging on to sin, we have chosen to shut a door to God's work in our lives. His Spirit is shut out of that area we were praying for peace or love or joy to grow in. Becoming aware of our "weeds," confessing them, and committing them to the Lord opens us up for His Spirit to move freely in us as He grows His bountiful harvest in our lives.

Read the following verses and journal the main idea in each:

Mark 6:5-6

_____

_____

Ephesians 4:30-32

_____

_____

Acts 7:51

_____

_____

1 Thessalonians 5:19-22

_____

_____

Hebrews 3:7-16

_____

_____

Hebrews 12:15 (the NAS translation of this verse gives more of a cause and effect reading than the NIV)

_____

_____

In the church today, we focus on God's love and grace. His love and grace are bigger than any of us can wrap our minds around. They deserve great attention! However, there is also a reality found in Scripture that God wants a relationship with His children; and in that relationship He has granted us freedom to harvest what we sow! We find it hard to balance the many facets of grace, love, truth and judgment. Regardless of how we humans might tend to be imbalanced in our approach to these theological subjects, they are all part of what makes up God's character.

The passages we studied today could most certainly leave us with heavy hearts. So I don't want us to close today's study quite yet! Read and personalize the following verses (you'll love these!):

Lamentations 3:20-23

_____

_____

Psalm 32:5-7

_____

_____

1 John 1:9

_____

_____

Recently, I confessed to a sister in the Lord how grieved I was over an issue God had brought to my attention. When the Lord spoke His correction gently into my heart, I was so ashamed at how I had ignored Him and gone my own way.

God is faithful to show us the places where we are broken; and He is faithful to fix us - amen? It isn't pretty to look at our failures, but it is good to watch our Father clean us up, isn't it? Open your heart freely to the One who loves you regardless of your mistakes, but who also loves you enough to make sure you don't keep living with the same old mistakes forever! Take the space below to write out your prayer and thoughts to Him:

_____

_____

_____

_____

_____

_____

_____

_____

_____

Day Four: Pests

When I was a kid I had a much greener thumb than I do now as an adult. Perhaps it was the soil where we lived or some other factor. Every year I would grow tomato and strawberry plants. I loved my plants! The first year I had my little garden my tomato plants were flourishing and healthy. As I watered them I noticed these large, green, alien-looking caterpillar things. They were *GI*-normous and like any sensible little eight year old girl, I yelled and got Dad to come to the rescue. He had never seen tomato bugs and he didn't quite know what to do with them either. So he plucked them off the plants and tossed them in the trash. (I mean they were so huge you'd have to have a proper burial for the body with a headstone if you tried to kill them!)

As a kid, I knew what to do about bugs - get Dad! As daughters of the Most High we can do the same thing for the invaders in our life that are out to destroy the harvest God wants in our heart.

The word *spirit* in Greek can refer to the Spirit of God, the spirit of man and a demonic spirit. If we study the fruit of the Spirit, only considering what the Holy Spirit does in our hearts, without considering what our broken nature is capable of producing (or the toll the enemy can take on our harvest), it is a very incomplete picture. Planting a garden without first preparing the soil or protecting the plants from outside issues like bugs or weather would be very unproductive. I think that is why, as Christians, we sometimes lack the victory God desires for us. We miss important pieces of the puzzle. (I am still looking around for a number of stray pieces in my own life!)

I sat down and wrote out the emotional opposite of each one of the traits of the fruit of the Spirit and here's what I came up with. (This is just how I keep my heart on the right track. I identify whatever *could* take me in the wrong direction and guard my life from it! This isn't Scripture, it's just one application of it! So don't get the idea that somewhere God laid down this set of fruit of the Spirit roadblocks. This is simply my own application of His Word as I share it with you.)

The opposite/hinderance of love in our lives could be hate/bitterness/unforgiveness.
The opposite/hinderance of joy in our lives could be despair/hopelessness.
The opposite/hinderance of peace in our lives could be anxiety/worry/fear.
The opposite/hinderance of patience in our lives could be anger
The opposite/hinderance of kindness in our lives could be criticalness.
The opposite/hinderance of goodness in our lives could be jealousy.
The opposite/hinderance of gentleness in our lives could be pride/arrogance (the Greek meaning of gentleness reveals a fuller meaning for this trait).
The opposite/hinderance of faithfulness in our lives could be doubt/faithlessness.

The opposite/hinderance of self-control in our lives could be self-indulgence/centeredness.

As we look over that list, what's our response to those ugly, opposing emotions? After all, they're just natural, human feelings, right? Yet these emotions stand in direct opposition to the work of the Holy Spirit in our hearts.

For the most part, good Christian girls who don't know what to do with those emotions, but also know they don't want to feel them, find a handy dandy coping mechanism. Things like pedicures, talking on the phone, eating ice cream, vegging on TV, getting a new hairdo, or shoes work for us (and really we've been trained to believe a new/right pair of shoes can change your life. It worked for Dorothy and Cinderella. So we just keep hoping we'll find the right shoes, don't we? It's like you can hardly even blame us!).

We do all those things and more. But those ugly emotions are still lurking in the hallways, waiting for a really stressful day or for us to be too tired to see them coming. Then they burst out and take center stage. Not only that, but those unresolved emotions can leave our lives open for a whole lot more than we bargained for.

Read these verses and paraphrase them in your own words. Identify how the enemy is kin to, close to, or in the midst of the negative emotions that come to us so naturally. I believe that this is how he stands in opposition to the fruit of the Spirit in our lives.

Look for love vs. bitterness - 2 Corinthians 2:10-11

_____

_____

_____

Look for joy vs. despair - John 10:10

_____

_____

_____

Look for peace vs. anxiety - 1 Peter 5:7-9

_____

_____

Look for patience vs. anger - Ephesians 4:26-27

_____

_____

_____

Look for kindness vs. criticalness - Revelation 12:10

_____

_____

_____

Look for goodness vs. jealousy/ambition - James 3:14-16

_____

_____

_____

Look for faithfulness vs. doubt - 1 Peter 5:8-9

_____

_____

_____

Look for gentleness vs pride - James 4:6-8

_____

_____

_____

Look for self-control versus self-indulgence - 1 Peter 5:8-9

_____

_____

_____

For me, it's a point of warning in **BIG BOLD LETTERS** that these natural emotions seem to always appear so closely to verses about the enemy in Scripture. I want my life as free from the influence and reach of the enemy as possible.

Years ago, around the time I started studying these connections, I was struggling with anger. I grew up around so much anger that it was in and around me, like a fish in water. The Lord led me to that verse from Ephesians 4 and gave me a fresh understanding for it.

In the version I'd always read, Satan is described as getting a "foothold" when we leave our hearts with unprocessed, lingering anger. A foothold, I imagined, was like shoving your foot in the door when someone is trying to shut it. So his foot in my door was not that big of a deal in my mind; and really not my fault. (I mean he's the one who shoved it there, right?) My understanding had been very wrong. A foothold is not getting a "foot in the door"; it is a military term. It's an outpost in enemy territory. In a more literal translation it reads that we "give place" to the devil with our unresolved anger. That is probably the better way to read this verse in order to help us in our struggle against the enemy.

Growing up, I lived in a small house with my parents and sisters. Everything happened in the kitchen. Meals, projects, laundry folding, homework, everything. And there was always something on the chairs and booth that encircled the busy table. So come dinner time we all would get called to clean off our homework, laundry, projects, etc. to make room for the next order of the day. Giving the devil a place is like moving a backpack off a kitchen chair so the enemy of our soul can have a place at the dinner table for a little chit chat. It's a bad thing. A serious thing. Not just an unintended, foot-in-the-door kind of thing.

It boggles my mind to think about how deeply our emotions can and *do* affect our spiritual health. It kind of freaks me out, in fact.

So there's a few things I prayerfully discovered how to do in order to process those snarky, weedy emotions so that the enemy can't get further mileage out of them.

As we continue this study together in weeks two through nine we'll learn:

1. The truth according to Scripture about God's fruitfulness and our emotions.

2. Understanding on how the fruit of the Spirit comes out of my being rooted in Christ and His character; and how understanding my identity in Christ enables me to grow in His likeness, rather than simply trying harder in my human strength to develop these qualities.

3. How to practically invite God's strength into my areas of weakness.

4. How to process natural, human emotions through obedience to God's word so that my unresolved emotions don't cheat me out of the good fruitfulness God desires for my life.

If you, like me, have allowed the enemy more freedom in various areas of your life than God intends, commit these areas to your heavenly Father. He will be faithful to come into the garden of your heart and shut out those ugly pests. Use some of the Scriptures we read through today to frame your Scripture prayers in the space below:

_____

_____

_____

_____

_____

_____

_____

_____

_____

Day Five: Taking Inventory

Soooo! This week we have looked at the parts and pieces of our heart garden. We have studied what fruitfulness looks like, the various soil conditions of the heart, the sin that can grow like weeds in our lives and the work of the enemy who devours our harvest like pests in a garden. Now it is time to take inventory of our current heart state!

Read the following verses and personalize each one:

Proverbs 4:23

_____

_____

Psalm 51:10, 17

_____

_____

Psalm 119:11

_____

_____

Ezekiel 36:26

_____

_____

Matthew 5:8

_____

_____

Journal your responses to each of the following questions:

1. Considering our study this week, are you actively guarding your heart from influences and issues that could quench the work of the Spirit in your heart? Is there an area where you think perhaps you need God to teach you how to guard it better?

_____

_____

_____

_____

2. Throughout our studies this week did you sense there were any areas in your heart that needed cleansing from the Lord? Have you asked God to cleanse those areas?

_____

_____

_____

_____

3. Look over your heart journal from the week. Ask God to reveal things about yourself and what He wants to do in your heart. Spend some time journaling and writing your own Scripture prayers.

_____

_____

_____

_____

_____

_____

Week Two
Your Love Life

. . . .

Day One
Defining Live

Day Two

Finding Yourself in the Center of God's Love

Day Three
His Strength in Your Weakness

Day Four
Love Through Forgiveness

Day Five
Called to be a Blessing

Key Verse:
A new commandment I give to you, that you love one another, even as I have loved you, that you also love one another. By this all men will know that you are My disciples, if you have love for one another. John 13:34-35

Day One: Defining Love

We walk through life with a host of concepts that create our picture of what it means to love and be loved. As a kid, I watched a lot of old movies. I lost count of how many times Rock Hudson lied, or Tony Curtis schmoozed something out of a girl (depending on the movie it was either affection, moola or both). John Wayne even spanked his wife in one movie (which in context was actually kinda funny--but the reality of it wouldn't be that humorous). The portrayal of love on the big screen leaves a lot to be desired--in both old and newer films. Even Disney movies depict love in some ways that aren't that great for kids. Did you ever notice that all the Disney princesses find their Prince Charming and ditch their parents when they are like 16??!! Well, enough with the movie tangent! Think on some of the positive and negative influences that have formed your concept of the various forms of love. Probably your parents relationship, friends, family, and church family have all played into this picture of love for you. Journal the words you might use to describe the feelings, actions and thoughts of love and then where you got that impression:

Romantic love

_____

_____

_____

_____

Platonic/ Friendship love

_____

_____

_____

_____

Parental love

_____

_____

_____

_____

I like to actually write these thoughts out on paper--when I do it makes me see them with greater clarity and take responsibility for them!

In Greek (which the New Testament was mostly written in) there are a variety of words that all translate into our English word love. Where many languages use three or four terms for "love," we have one. So I love my puppy and my cat, I love tacos and guacamole, I love my sisters and I love my husband...love all the way around with no linguistic distinction between the different scenarios. In Greek, however, there are distinctions between the words you would use in each of those situations. In the New Testament there are two primary forms of the word love used--*agapao* and *phileo*. *Agapao* is a moral love that puts the needs of the other person before the one giving the love. It is a love that sacrifices for the good of others. *Phileo* is a warm, fuzzy, affectionate love. One that is based in and expressed through the emotions. The fruit of the spirit passage (Galatians 5:22-24) which we are studying uses the agape form of the word.

Now, let's dig into some of the ways God defines love. Read the following verses and journal the main idea of each. Next to each of the verses I wrote *agape* or *phileo* next to the reference to give you an extra sense of the way God defines love in each situation.

General love
John 13:34-35 (agape)

_____

_____

Romans 5:8 (agape)

_____

_____

1 Corinthians 8:1 (agape)

_____

_____

1 Peter 4:8 (agape)

_____

_____

1 John 4:18 (agape)

_____

_____

Romantic love

Proverbs 5 (if you have teens--this is a great passage to discuss with them because it shows God's heart for us to enjoy romantic love)

_____

_____

Ephesians 5:25 (agape)

_____

_____

Titus 2:4 (phileo)

_____

_____

Friendship love

Proverbs 17:17

_____

_____

John 15:13-14 (agape)

_____

_____

John 13:35 (agape)

_____

_____

Romans 12:10-11 (mentions both kinds of love)

_____

_____

Philippians 2:1-2 (agape--the context is church relationships)

_____

_____

1 Thessalonians 4:9-10 (mentions both forms of love)

_____

_____

Parental love
Psalm 27:10

_____

_____

Isaiah 49:15-16

_____

_____

Ephesians 1:4-5 (agape)

_____

_____

If you were to rate how you have been loving on those around you (based on the Scriptural definition), on a scale of one (being the lowest) to ten (being the highest) where would you fall? Circle the level you would rate some of the closest relationships to your heart and write the name of the person (or their initials) next to the circled number.

1   2   3   4   5   6   7   8   9   10

Write some of the verses from today's study on your Scripture prayer cards and spend some time dialoging with the Lord about His definition of love and His vision for how He wants you to live His love out loud in your life for everyone to see.

<u>*Day Two: Finding yourself in the center of God's love*</u>

Today's topic is one of my most favorite Bible study topics! It is the one topic that changed my life the most--and an area where God is still working on me! We are going to dive into Scriptures that reveal God's heart of love for us, how He sees us and how all that completely changes our lives!

Pull out your "Who I am in Christ" list and begin by reading through those Scriptures. Which attributes are hard to identify with? Why?

Now read and personalize the following verses:

Psalm 45:11

_____

_____

Psalm 138:8

_____

_____

Psalm 139:14

_____

_____

Song of Solomon 2:14

_____

_____

Isaiah 43:1-4

_____

_____

Isaiah 62:3-5

_____

_____

Jeremiah 31:3-4 (note--God had referred to the people of Israel earlier in the book as spiritual harlots because of the way they loved and chased after other gods. Based on this verse, how does God see us and our sin when we have repented from our waywardness?)

_____

_____

Zephaniah 3:17

_____

_____

When I have my identity rooted in God's love for me, His love flows through me to others more readily. When I am rooted in His love, I am emotionally secure. I don't walk around with an empty emotional cup looking for someone to fill it, because my Lord already has! That sense of security frees me up to love others--and it frees me from the wounds others have inflicted on my heart. (We will talk more about how wounds get in the way of loving others in more depth on days four and five.)

Write some more Scripture prayers from the verses you looked up today. Spend some time dialoging with the Lord over His love for you!

_____

_____

_____

_____

_____

_____

_____

_____

_____

Day Three: His Strength in my Weakness

Every week of this study we will devote one day to studying the character of God as it relates to the topic of the week. We will focus on His strength and ask for Him to come into our particular area of weakness with His power and ability. In relation to loving others--it is a real stretch for us to lavishly love the difficult or hurtful people in our lives. But with God's strength and His wisdom we can learn how to love people in healthy, fruitful ways regardless of how they treat us.

Read the following verses and write the main idea of each one:

Psalm 36:6

_____

_____

Psalm 63:3

_____

_____

Nehemiah 9:17

_____

_____

John 3:13

_____

_____

Romans 5:8

_____

_____

Romans 8:38-39

_____

_____

Titus 3:4

_____

_____

1 John 3:1

_____

_____

1 John 3:16

_____

_____

1 John 4:16

_____

_____

When I was being discipled I learned a great habit. When you're tripping over yourself (like I do, constantly!) it is good to write down what specific issues you are tripping over. Is it that your mouth shoots off, are you struggling to forgive, does being critical come too easily for you, etc. Take a piece of paper and make two columns. On one side write out your junk. Then use a concordance and look up verses that describe God's character as the very opposite of the quality your struggling with. Write the verse in the other column. Confess your uglies to God and ask His strength to fill that nasty hole in you. Ask Him to make you keenly aware of the issue in you and, if you're willing, ask Him to make you just as sick over that particular sin in you as it makes Him. He always answers that last part for me with such swiftness and faithfulness! But truly, do we want to be women to cling to our sins or chuck 'em over board and cling to our Lord? God's taken some mighty interesting measures to root sin out of me and I'm thankful for it, even if it wasn't pleasant.

Here's a chart you can use to begin honing in on God's love in place of your weakness:

Your Love Weakness	God's Love Filling Strength

Now read Ephesians 3:16 and make it the start of your prayer time! (Isn't that a great verse?) Use the verses you looked up to form your Scripture prayers asking for His "glorious riches [that] He might strengthen you with power through His Spirit in your inner being!"

_____

_____

_____

_____

_____

_____

_____

_____

_____

_____

_____

Day Four: Called to Forgive

Read the following verses and write the pros and cons of choosing to forgive or not forgive:

Matthew 5:7

_____

_____

Matthew 6:14-15

_____

_____

Matthew 18:21-35

_____

_____

Luke 6:37 (While this passage is very important to our topic, I often hear it misused...the word *condemn* in that circumstance indicated judging the person--not just the action--passing a sentence on them, and punishing them. It's not wrong to wisely discern the fruit of someone's life.)

_____

_____

Summarize the points from the above verses in the chart below:

When I choose...

	To Forgive	Not to Forgive
Good stuff that happens in my life		
Bad stuff that happens in my life		

*Note about Matthew 18:21-35: A talent was a value of money. According to Barnes Notes[3], one talent was equivalent to about three thousand shekels and one shekel was worth about fifty cents. Now the one slave owed the other one hundred denarii. The denarius (singular form of denarii) was a common coin that, according to Barnes' studies, would be equal to about fifteen cents. So the one slaved owed about fifteen dollars, compared to the debt to the master of about $15,000,000! Now there's a picture for ya! If I were to take an honest account of all my sins and count up the debt, I am afraid there would be no end to it. When I get stuck on the offenses of those around me it is like choking that person and throwing her/him into prison (or wanting to) for a fifteen dollar favor. When you owe that much and have been released of the debt, you ought to be able to cast a little grace in another's direction.

Below is a very practical picture for processing forgiveness from Pam and Bill Farrel:
1. I forgive (name) for (offense).
2. I admit that what was done was wrong.
3. I do not expect (name) to make up for what s/he did.
4. I will not use this offense to manipulate (name).
5. I will not use this offense to define (name).
6. I will not allow the offense to stop my personal growth.[4]

Pam discipled me and while under her wing, I had those steps to forgiveness taped all over my world. I had a lot of baggage to sort through and most of it needed to go in the "forgiveness" pile. As broken thoughts and emotions would surface I would go through that list, sometimes even out loud, over and over. Rinse and repeat. Forgiveness is a process. Someone can wound you once, but the pain ripples and reverberates over the surface of your soul. Each time the waters of your heart stir over an offense, just go through those forgiveness steps. It doesn't mean you didn't forgive them yesterday, it just means you feel the wound today. Injuries to the heart are no different than a physical sore that needs to be re-bandaged, dressed and cleaned more than once. Eventually, with the right "medicine" your wounds will heal and they won't dictate your emotions.

Use the Scriptures from today's lesson to write your Scripture prayers and pray through any places in your heart that might be harboring unforgiveness.

_____

_____

_____

_____

_____

_____

Day Five: Called to be a Blessing

Read and personalize 1 Peter 3:8-9:

_____

_____

_____

_____

When we think of a calling on someone's life we most often envision grandiose plans--like being the next Billy Graham, the President of the United States or some other high profile kind of position. Maybe we have an eternal perspective on the labor of love poured over the task of mothering, teaching Sunday school or praying for our neighbors that gives us a sense of calling. But most of us don't automatically think of blessing-those-who-have-hurt-us as our "high calling" in life. Yet this is the very calling Peter speaks of in the above verses. We were called by God to be a blessing to the very people who have wounded us!

Read and paraphrase
Matthew 5:44

_____

_____

_____

Romans 12:14, 17-21

_____

_____

_____

_____

1 Corinthians 4:12-13

_____

_____

1 Thessalonians 5:15

_____

_____

_____

It is a tall order, isn't it? I mean it is one thing to forgive those who have hurt us (like we studied previously), but it is a whole different ball game when we start talking about going out of our way to *bless* them! The word *bless* in the Greek means to speak well of someone. The Lord wants our hearts free from the entanglements of bitterness, so He instructs us to forgive. He desires His children to be vessels of blessing, just as He was, so He teaches us to bless those who have hurt us. But He never asks us to hang good sense on the doorpost and walk into a situation we know will bring us further pain or abuse. So where is the balance in this? Honestly, I have a hard time finding it myself. But there have been two definite ways the Lord has impressed on my heart to carry out His design for me to be a blessing to those who have wounded me. Both ways have to do with speaking well of the other person.

1. **Speak well of them in public**. If I am in a group setting and the person in question comes up in conversation I will try my best to say something positive (still being genuine while I say it) about him/her. And if I can't think of anything good to say, well, you know the old adage--if you can't say anything nice, don't say anything at all. Sometimes we need to process our hurt verbally, but there is a private time and place for that. Ninety-nine percent of the time it isn't our opportunity to verbally process our records of wounds when it disgraces another.

2. **Pray blessings over them**. I have certain Scripture passages from the New Testament that I rephrase into a prayer of blessing over the person who has hurt me. Sometimes I pray them out of obedience and ask God to align my heart with His Word. Sometimes the prayers of blessing flow freely from my heart. I have always found that if I am faithful in this process, God is faithful to put a genuine desire in my heart for the other person to be deeply blessed.

Rewrite these verses into prayers of blessing for someone in your life who might qualify for today's topic of study:

Ephesians 1:17-19

_____

_____

_____

_____

Philippians 1:9-11

_____

_____

_____

_____

Romans 15:13

_____

_____

John 8:31-32

_____

_____

_____

Colossians 3:15

_____

_____

_____

It's OK to pray, "Lord, I am praying these blessings in obedience to your desire for me to bless those who have hurt me--but I am asking you to change my heart in accordance with Your Word so that my heart would freely echo Your Word." Whenever I begin this process of praying blessings over someone who has hurt me--it is VERY hard. Over time though, it becomes a genuine desire for me to see God bless them! And I am thrilled when I see how He answers these prayers and truly blesses them.

The ultimate sign of forgiveness is the desire to see blessing fill the other person's life. Recently I watched as the person who has hurt me more than any other person in my life received a deep blessing in their life. I had even prayed for this specific blessing to come about for many years. But I was not prepared for the way the blessing would be smeared in my face and the renewed sense of wounding I would experience. The best I could do in the situation was to pray for God's favor, grace and hand to cover this person. I did not divulge my wounds in a way that would disgrace this individual. It hurt. Deeply. And while the Lord called me to be involved in the situation for a season, He did not require that I expose my heart unnecessarily. I desire the best for this person. And can walk free from the hurts only when I give them fully to God and His grace. May you find His grace near enough and big enough to fulfill your calling to be a blessing to those who have hurt you. It is in taking this narrow and high road that we receive an inheritance of blessing from our Father in heaven (1 Peter 3:9)

Write any additional thoughts to the Lord:

_____

_____

_____

_____

_____

_____

_____

_____

_____

_____

Week Three
Where's the Joy, Joy, Joy Down in my Heart?

· ·

Day One
A Joy Worth Fighting For

Day Two
Joy in How God Sees Me

Day Three
His Strength in My Weakness

Day Four
Cultivating Joy

Day Five
Living Joy out Loud

Key Verse:
These things I have spoken to you so that My joy may be in you, and that your joy may be made full. John 15:11

Day One: A Joy Worth Fighting For

God has so many awesome promises for His children. The fact of the matter is that quite often His kids don't even know all the promises made to them, let alone how to activate those promises. But even worse yet, the enemy knows every one of God's promises and does his very best to keep God's children from experiencing the harvest of joy and fullness designed for them. Read and personalize each one of the following verses:

John 10:10

_____

_____

John 16:24

_____

_____

John 17:13

_____

_____

Romans 14:17

_____

_____

Psalm 5:11

_____

_____

Psalm 30:5

_____

_____

Isaiah 51:11

_____

_____

Nehemiah 8:10

_____

_____

Clearly, our joy--or lack thereof--is very important to our Father in Heaven. Joy is the fruit of the victory He has won in our lives. It's a sign for others to see in our hearts for His glory. All this to say, joy is a crucial part of our testimony. One of the startling facets of the early Christians' testimony to the world was their joy that trumped the torture and death they met head on. Satan wants our joy to be silenced.

Think about a time that should have been joyful, but wasn't very joyful for you. Journal your experience and what you think might have been going on in your life. Ask God to help you sort through the details.

_____

_____

_____

_____

_____

_____

_____

Look up Revelation 12:11. Based on this verse, what two things overcome Satan:

_____

Joy is a flag of victory, the waving story of our testimony to God's power, redemption, love and grace. No wonder Satan wants our joy to be extinguished! Spend some time in prayer asking God to grow His joy in your heart; joy with strong roots to weather the storms of life. I am praying His joy to grow more in all of our hearts!

_____

_____

_____

_____

_____

_____

_____

_____

_____

_____

_____

_____

_____

_____

_____

_____

_____

<u>*Day Two: Joy in How God Sees Me*</u>

Psalm 51:12 speaks of the "joy of my salvation." I grew up in a home where the concepts of salvation were taught--something I am very grateful for. So I honestly don't remember a time in my life when I didn't trust in Jesus' sacrifice for my mistakes and sins--which I knew were plentiful. But I really experienced the joy of my salvation for the first time during the season that God opened my eyes to how He saw me. His Word utterly blew my mind when I allowed His Spirit to press it into my heart. My mentor had given me the assignment to read the "Who I am in Christ" list from the New Testament three times a day, like a spiritual meal. At first I read it with an attitude of "Isn't this great for all those nice, pretty church ladies, but God doesn't really mean this for me." His Spirit convicted me. This wasn't a matter of "feeling" this was a matter of belief. I could believe my crummy mantra or I could believe God's word. I could believe the world's words or my Maker's. It was a choice of faith. Slowly, I began to absorb His truth. Then I looked up passages from the Old Testament that revealed general aspects to how God sees His children. Wow! The way God sees us is light years away from the way I generally feel about myself. Regardless of how I might naturally think about myself (or how you might think about yourself), it is the Creator who gets to define His creation, not the other way around!

Read and personalize the following verses:

Psalm 45:11

_____

_____

Philippians 4:13

_____

_____

Romans 8:31, 37-39

_____

_____

Ephesians 2:10

_____

_____

When I lose my joy and start down the slippery path to the pit of despair, my internal dialogue (uninterrupted by God's Word) goes something like this--*You are such a dummy! You always mess everything up! You are such a stinking failure! What is the matter with you? Will you ever get yourself together? You are a waste of oxygen!!!*

Well, you get the point--it isn't pretty stuff going on in my head--how 'bout yours? God, the perfect One, doesn't think those things about me or anyone else--and if anyone has the right to say/think those kind of things, it would be Him! Instead, He says through His grace that you (and I) are beautiful, capable in His strength, never separated from His absolute, complete love, and His very workmanship--His masterpiece. So if the Lord, the Only Perfect One, doesn't rant on and on about our messy house, how late we were to that appointment, how our figure isn't what it used to be or any of the rest of it, who are we to rant the way we do?

Read and personalize John 8:32

_____

_____

The word for free is *eleutheroo* (el-yoo-ther-o'o). It means to be free or exempt from liability. The adjective form of the word means "freedom from restraint and obligation." If I know, believe, act on and live in the truth about the way God sees me I am liberated and free from living under the restraint of my failures, my weakness and my depression. I may struggle--yes. But I don't owe my failures any more of my life than they already have taken--move forward. I don't owe my bad memories anymore of my life than they already robbed me of--move forward. I don't owe my weaknesses any more than to commit them to Christ--no wallowing in them. I don't owe the darkness of depression one ounce of territory in my life--I am moving forward into Christ's love and that is growing a harvest of joy in this soul!

Spend some time using the Scripture passages we've studied so far to create a few Scripture prayers.

_____

_____

_____

_____

_____

_____

_____

_____

_____

_____

_____

_____

_____

_____

_____

_____

_____

<u>Day Three: His Strength in My Weakness</u>

Read Hebrews 4:15 and personalize that verse:

_____

_____

It is a comfort to know that when I am struggling with an emotionally gray (or black) day, Jesus looks upon my weakness with sympathy. Check out these verses and paraphrase each one:

Read Isaiah 53:3-4

_____

_____

Matthew 26:37-38

_____

_____

Luke 19:41-42

_____

_____

Hebrews 5:7

_____

_____

Jesus had His share of reasons to be depressed while He traveled the dusty roads of this earth. And His view from heaven isn't perkier either. He has witnessed every travesty and horror this world has experienced since the dawn of time. Psalm 56 tells us that He collects all of our tears--and I am sure that He collects them with concern, compassion and empathy. So our Lord can well identify with the burdens of our hearts. Yet, the difference between His sorrow and mine (and perhaps yours as well) is that He was never mastered by the burden of His sorrow.

Read and paraphrase 1 Corinthians 6:12

_____

_____

Jesus doesn't want us to be plastic Christians with smiles glued on when life is ripping our hearts apart. But He does want us to reap a harvest of joy in our lives, even when life is hard.

Read and paraphrase the following verses:

Hebrews 12:2-3

_____

_____

James 1:2-4

_____

_____

Matthew 5:10

_____

_____

Luke 6:22-23

_____

_____

Acts 5:41

_____

_____

Romans 8:17

_____

_____

2 Corinthians 12:9-10 (the NIV uses the word "delight"--I like that translation for this

verse)

_____

_____

1 Peter 4:13

_____

_____

Spend some time writing the verses that have meant the most to you on your 3 X 5 cards into more Scripture prayers--or just write the verses. Dialogue with the Lord over the burdens in your heart and the joy that He wants to grow in the midst of them.

<u>*Day Four: Cultivating Joy*</u>

Above all else, guard your heart because from it flow the issues of life. Proverbs 4:23

In our journey with the Lord to have hearts of soft soil without weeds for Him to freely work in, we must also be aware of what we allow into the garden of our hearts. We have to be on guard against things that distract or hinder His work in our lives. When cultivating joy, we must be careful of "joy suckers".

Eric and I attended a conference a few months before we were married where we heard pastor H. B. London give a very honest message about what he referred to as the "joy suckers" in life. He shared about crabby parishioners that cared more about the weeds growing between the asphalt cracks in the parking lot than the growth of individuals and ministries in the church. He shared about people and circumstances that sucked the joy and focus of ministry right out from under him and hard trials in life that knocked the wind out of him. Listening to this older man in ministry share so honestly was a huge encouragement! It's nice to know you're not alone--and his seasoned wisdom became an important part in our pursuits to serve the Lord. He wisely stated that God allows joy suckers into our lives so that we will grow thick skin, deep roots and maturity. He said they also serve as a reminder that we are serving God's agenda, not man's and so we can't look to people for approval. While life has it's share of joy suckers, sometimes it is us who hold the most responsibility for allowing the influences of people and things into our lives that God never intended.

Read the following verses and note the influences within and without that leaned on these godly men until their spirits were crushed:

Numbers 11:10-15

_____

_____

1 Kings 19:1-8

_____

_____

Job 10 (the whole chapter)

_____

_____

Psalm 42

_____

_____

Jonah 3:10-4:4

_____

_____

2 Corinthians 1:8-11

_____

_____

Can you relate to the emotions these heroes of the faith struggled with? I know I can! Journal about which story resonated most with your heart and why.

_____

_____

_____

_____

_____

As I journeyed to a place with God where depression no longer mastered me, He led me to take an inventory of my life and see what kind of behavior patterns were associated with my slumps. I also studied those passages we just read to see what triggered the hopelessness of other God-followers in Scripture. Moses was angry and overwhelmed, Job was beside himself with grief, Jonah was bitter and angry, Elijah was physically worn out and anxious, David was running for his life, and Paul had pressures of every sort plaguing his ministry.

So I kept a journal to monitor my habits and what brought me to the place of despair. Before a slump I was often physically exhausted and because of that tired state I would let go of taking care of personal balance and health. I would get messy and unorganized because I didn't take the time to care for my personal space. Being unorganized made me frustrated with myself, rushed (as I never could find the things I needed) and reinforced my negative thoughts about myself and my capabilities. Because I was tired and hurried I would let go of personal hygiene and "fixing myself up." And because I felt so tired and busy, I withdrew from people because I felt I didn't have time for friendships. Overload was a big depression initiator for me. God led me to do 180 degree turns against my knee jerk responses which only reinforced the negativity and despair I was feeling. So when I felt like laying in a lump, I made myself drink a big glass of water and get outside for a walk, clean my room or office, take a long bubble bath and wear a pretty skirt--even if I hated it every step along the way. I would do this day after day until the cloud lifted and I found that the more I dialogued with God over my feelings and habits, and obeyed His leading, the less and less that nasty cloud came around. I also had issues with unforgiveness, anger and other emotions that left me vulnerable to enemy attack. God and I had a long journey through those messy emotional pits until they were resolved--or resolved to a healthier place. Another thing that I have noticed is the people I hang around with make a big difference in cultivating joy in my life. Being around spiritually and emotionally healthy/growing people is like fertilizer for joy in the soul. They encourage me, pray for me, express concern for me and correct me out of love. Spending time around people who put others down to feel better about themselves is always a downer for me--not a depresser kind of thing--but a definite joy sucker. People who are bent on criticism, comparing, competition or confrontation just for the sake of the drama or control are all people I need to be around only in limited doses.

What are the joy suckers you need to guard against? Consider your life habits and write down things that make joy-cracks in your heart:

_____

_____

_____

_____

What 180 degree turns do you need to make away from the joy suckers in your life? Maybe the Lord is laying something on your heart right now, maybe you need to pray over it for a while to know better what to do. Write what is on your heart.

_____

_____

_____

_____

_____

_____

Proverbs 3:18 says, "She [wisdom] is a tree of life to those who take hold of her, and happy are all who hold her fast." May God grant you wisdom and the grace to hold on to it so that you might find the joy of soul that God designed to grow in your heart.

Day Five: Living Joy out Loud

Praising God is the ultimate form of joy for the Christian. But praise isn't just the stuff we do when we are singing in church on Sunday. Worshipping God is wide and deep. It's an attitude we carry around with us at all times.

Recently, I was really convicted over my lack of gratitude. For a variety of reasons life has conditioned me to always keep my eye out for the stuff that is amiss, the things that need fixing...basically to be overly analytical...alright! *critical*! If we had hours to chat over coffee, you'd understand how my life-vision got shaped this way and I'd learn how yours might have too. I confess, it comes far too naturally to me and it has been reinforced until it has utterly become a second language to me. As a pastor's wife, I constantly have my eye out for who might feel left out, who might need extra TLC, who might not be all that safe, who needs what, etc. My eyes get fixed on the holes and potential holes in church-life and that way of thinking lobs into the rest of life too. Lately God has been convicting me of the deep ways this affects my precious man. I never meant for it to...it just sort of happened.

That tendency to spot issues and snags acts like a drain on my heart's joy and gratitude. It serves to agitate my heart like wind on a lake. I know my husband would love to see my heart in a place of genuine peace and stillness--God would too (Psalm 46:10)! And I'm starting to see gratitude as a serious missing link to maintaining that spirit of quiet trust. I've always been grateful for the simple pleasures in life, but there's more to gratitude than saying "Thanks" to God or others. It's a constant heartbeat that doesn't leave room for frustrations, irritations, or eyes that look for the "holes" in life. Gratitude and joy can't fit in the same heart space as mistrust, unthankfulness, a need for control, or fear. As we've studied this week, joy is a flying flag of our testimony and worship is the pinnacle of that joy in our Father.

Read and personalize the following verses. As you do, write one practical way you can implement this in your day/week/life in general.

Psalm 30:11-12

_____

_____

Psalm 9:1

_____

_____

Psalm 26:7

_____

_____

Psalm 34:1

_____

_____

Psalm 40:2-3

_____

_____

Psalm 42:5

_____

_____

Psalm 106:1-2

_____

_____

Psalm 79:13

_____

_____

Colossians 3:16

_____

_____

Praising God involves what we say, what we sing, our attitude as we live life, and even a little dancing in there too! Can you imagine how awesome our corporate worship would be if we were all cultivating hearts of praise the rest of the week? I want to be a woman of joy and praise to my God! I know you do too! Let's all pray for the work God has, is, and will do in each other's lives in this area!

_____

_____

_____

_____

_____

_____

_____

_____

_____

_____

Week Four

An All Surpassing Peace

. . . .

Day One
In Pursuit of Peace

Day Two
Our Prince of Peace

Day Three
His Strength in my Weakness

Day Four
Peaceful Steps

Day Five
Peace Under Fire

Key Verse:
"Peace I leave with you; My peace I give to you; not as the world gives do I give to you. Do not let your heart be troubled, nor let it be fearful."

John 14:27

Day One: In Pursuit of Peace

When you think of the word *peace*, what comes to mind? When was the last time you truly felt at peace? Write your thoughts here:

_____

_____

_____

_____

_____

_____

_____

Most of us live activity-packed, deadline-driven lives that lack peace. Even little kids have schedules that run them ragged. When I was a Children's Director I remember one little girl telling me she wasn't sure she would be able to memorize the week's Bible verse because her schedule was so packed she didn't think she could fit one more thing in! Peace eludes us. Quietness and stillness are foreign to us. Yet this is not the way God designed it to be.

Read and personalize the following verses:

Philippians 4:7

_____

_____

John 14:27

_____

_____

John 16:33

_____

_____

I want that kind of peace! Beyond all the lifestyle and dietary changes we should all probably make to lower stress on our systems, the Lord holds out lasting, stable, permeating peace to us. Yet, of all the facets of His fruitfulness in us, whether it's just busyness or extreme anxiety, I think peace is the one that the enemy presses in hardest against. It requires so much effort and diligence to cultivate peace, doesn't it? Sometimes I feel like instead of a cup to hold the fresh peace the Lord pours into me, I have a sieve. It runs out far too easily and quickly; and then I'm back again asking for more.

The Greek word for *peace* in the Galatians fruit of the Spirit passage is *eirene*, which means *quietness, prosperity and rest*. It also means *oneness*. The verb form literally means *to join*.[1] I think peace is slippery because true peace comes from being wholly and completely joined with Christ; and while we are spiritually and positionally joined with Christ, practically being joined with Christ is a moment by moment tug-of-war. We have to be utterly lost in Him to be wrapped in consistent peace; and it's far to easy to get lost in the demands of the moment, the relationships that painfully tug at our hearts, and the disappointments lurking in the corners of our minds.

What's the biggest thing right now that kills your peace? Is there a time of day that you worry more in than others? Is there something that triggers nerves or fears? Confess what you've allowed, intentionally or unintentionally, to steal away from Christ's work of peace in your heart.

_____

_____

_____

One last verse to close us out and hang onto as we ponder our peace-drains; look up Psalm 55:18 and personalize it:

_____

_____

_____

Now, take three 3X5 cards and write out three verses from today's study. It's only three verses, but marinate in them. These verses describe some of the work that Jesus suffered and died to accomplish in our hearts. Spend some deep time with Him praying over what might be keeping you from receiving this work to the fullest measure. Write out your heart and prayers on the lines provided below:

_____

_____

_____

_____

_____

_____

_____

_____

_____

_____

_____

_____

Day Two: Our Prince of Peace

Each facet of the fruit of the Spirit is cultivated from God and His character within us. Practically, I think this takes shape in two ways in our day-to-day living (I'm sure there's more than two, these two are just the two I've used most and fit our study best).

The first is having our identity totally wrapped up and rooted in Christ. When we allow our Creator to define who we are, instead of allowing our circumstances, our failings (or even successes), or our own self-image define us, God's power comes into our lives.

The second practical way to tap into God's character is to be constantly and keenly aware of how very *not* God we are. Instead, as those ugly weaknesses rear their heads, we ought to immediately confess them and ask for God's specific strength of character to fill the void in our hearts. We'll repeat these two concepts again and again for each fruit of the Spirit quality.

In terms of developing peace in our lives, rooting our identity in Christ is absolutely pivotal. Just consider how often feelings of insecurity steal away from peace in your heart.

I heard a woman speaker for a group of moms discuss the idea that all our fussing about needing to lose weight, in the end, might not be pleasing to the Lord. She went on to say that maybe He would rather that heart space be spent worshiping Him, or praying, or cultivating stillness in our spirit so we can learn to respond better to the prompting of the Holy Spirit when He is directing us.

We almost take beating ourselves up for granted! I've spent countless hours beating myself up over legitimate and feared mistakes. When I think of the fact that God has eternal, Kingdom work for me to do and this fussing isn't productive in the least bit, it startles some sense into me.

If you and I want lives with strong testimonies for Jesus in us and through us, we're going to have to ditch a lot of the "us" part. He must increase and we must decrease. That is true even in regard to how we see ourselves. Me and my perspective have just got to go because there isn't room or time for God's truth *and* mine to keep battling it out in me. You and I have bigger and better things to be about doing and thinking and feeling than this same old cyclical struggle. We've got peace waiting for us as soon as we let go of our inward wrestling.

Read and personalize the following verses (some will be repeats from this same exercise in earlier lessons, but they are so applicable, we can't skip over them. And truth be told, we need to revisit them and hear the Lord speak His word over us again and again for it to truly be planted in us and bear fruit through us. So here goes!):

Romans 8:15-17

_____

_____

Psalm 27:10

_____

_____

Psalm 68:5

_____

_____

Psalm 146:9

_____

_____

Hosea 2:19

_____

_____

John 15:13-17

_____

_____

_____

Song of Solomon 2:14

_____

_____

Zephaniah 3:17

_____

_____

Relationships are very important to most of us. Depending on your personality, they could be the most important facet of your life. Relationships can be sources of sweetness, joy, and actual stress-relief as we share burdens and get encouragement from others. However, they can also be devastating, vexing and *very* stressful. Before I proceed into the next idea about relationships and our identities in Christ, I want to make a little side-note.

For years I whole-heartedly believed that it takes two to tango, as the saying goes, to make a relationship succeed or fail. Throw my strong beliefs in with a few more years of weathering, experience and watching some very dear loved ones act out in hurtful ways, and I now have a new thought on the matter.

Yes, it takes two. Ninety percent of the time we are equally at fault in a relationship issue. So we can't bury ourselves in these promises of God when we are acting blatantly, actively and unrepentantly against them. It's crazy-making to say to yourself "If Mom and Dad push me out God will hold me and I'll be His! I don't need them!" If Mom and Dad pushed you out because you wouldn't stop bringing drugs into the house, lying, stealing from them, or bringing some other sort of trauma on them, that sort of response would fitting. However, sometimes our parents are so lost in their own troubles that we really need our Father in heaven to call us His, adopt us and give us a place in His family.

Sometimes we've been great friends to really not-so-great friends. It's true that if you give 100%, the relationship will be at least 50% better. But it is also true that sometimes the relationships we pour our 100% into just aren't healthy, God honoring ones, no matter how much we wish they were. Coming to that realization has been hard for me, and maybe hard for you too.

A dear friend of mine has the sweetest child...I mean truly a glowing, beautiful, amazing girl. Her husband left the two of them and went on a rampage of unthinkable decisions. He left his two beautiful girls for a very ugly life. I know their family and my "it-takes-two" theory doesn't hold up. I've known sweet, beautiful (knock 'em dead beautiful) women who were left by cheating husbands. They had been supportive, respectful women who loved being wives and loved their husbands. Sweet, loving, beautiful people are abused, cheated on, and abandoned every day and they sadly absorb those wounds into their own identity.

I've walked through a few toxic relationships. And they have left my heart tattered. I had tried everything, given everything and been broken. They were causes of massive stress for me. Our lives have ties on them we don't always choose and when those ties are toxic, they are wildly painful.

For relationships that are akin to peace "black-holes," see what Scripture has to say:

Proverbs 29:9

_____

_____

Ecclesiastes 10:12-13

_____

_____

_____

Matthew 7:6

_____

_____

John 2:24-25

_____

_____

Romans 16:17

_____

_____

Proverbs 6:16

_____

_____

Proverbs 4:23

_____

_____

While Scripture instructs us to turn the other cheek and go the extra mile, God also warns us to guard our hearts against people who are bent on division, lying, arrogance, and arguing. A person can start out merely speaking rashly or foolishly; but in the end his or her words can bring "wicked madness" to our relationship and our lives.

While Jesus did not withhold even His lifeblood from us, He also didn't blindly or ignorantly give His heart to the crowds who just wanted to see more miracles (see John 2:24-25).

Growing up I could not understand how Jesus could say that we could figuratively give our "pearls" to swinish people. It seemed so harsh to me. And if we repeated it to the person, it would be. But in wisdom, discernment and leaning heavily into the Holy Spirit's leading, these verses of relationship caution are meant for us to obey. Satan is ruthless and tireless in his efforts to rip off God's fruitfulness in our lives. If we constantly invite unsafe people into our close lives, which Scripture warns us against, the gardens of our hearts will lose their peace as the evil one pockets what God wants in our hearts.

At times, the pain from those peace-robbing relationships has very much threatened to completely overtake my identity in Christ. It is in those moments I desperately needed God's Word in me. When we, daughters of God, feel as if our very name is "Hurt," "Left," "Divorced," "Used," "Damaged," "Dirty," "Failure," "Hopeless,"

"Broken," "Brought-This-On-Yourself," what we really need is God's truth to free us from those lies and make us His. In His grace and mercy, God has made us Holy and Whole in Christ, Redeemed, Clean, Healed, Free, Hope and Dearly Beloved.

Your value is not reflected in how you've been treated. Who you are is not what has been done to you. Just because someone said it, doesn't make it truth. You belong to God - no one else. Nothing else. He is your loving, unfailing Father. He is your Husband in the Spirit and His heart towards you is steadfast, lasting, unfailing love and kindness. Jesus is your friend who laid down His life; you could never be alone.

You have been chosen by God Himself. Let Him hear your voice, lift your face to Him because your voice is sweet and your face is lovely to Him (see Song of Solomon 2:14). Let His love over you subdue the wrestling of your soul and His lullaby of love quiet your heart. There is peace of soul here and only here.

Day Three: His Strength in My Weakness

As we seek to cultivate peace (*eirene:* "oneness with Christ"), inviting His strength into our weakness is crucial. We've talked about what, when and who might be peace-drains on our hearts; and discussed how maintaining a perspective rooted in Biblical truth can plug up those holes. Today's study is another piece of "hole-plugging!"

Take your list of peace robbing thoughts and ask God to show you what's at the root of them. Many times there is some sort of sneaky sin hiding under something that looks benign, like worry. If you don't have one already, purchase a good concordance and put it to use!

When finances worry me, it's because I'm not trusting in God's faithful provision. So I find verses about His provision, confess my doubting, and ask God to fill me with confidence in Him. When I'm worrying over some situation, sometimes it's because I don't have control over it. God's the One who is in control, not me. I confess my pitiful control issues. I pray for God to make my soul "Be still and know that He is God." Sometimes life is just so taxing that peace eludes me and it is in those moments I simply pray for my Prince of Peace to reign in, and over, my heart and life.

So, take some moments to do the same! To start you off, here's some verses about God's character that have brought peace to my heart. Hopefully they will bring peace to yours as well. Some of these verses are very specific to a person or situation in Scripture. However, a piece of God's timeless character is revealed in each instance.

Look these verses up and personalize them:

Genesis 15:1 (I really like the NIV translation)

_____

_____

Genesis 16:13

_____

_____

Genesis 22:14

_____

_____

Exodus 15:26

_____

_____

Leviticus 20:8

_____

_____

Judges 6:24

_____

_____

Psalm 23:1

_____

_____

Matthew 1:23

_____

_____

John 6:35

_____

_____

John 7:37

_____

_____

John 8:11

_____

_____

John 10:10

_____

_____

John 16:33

_____

_____

These verses comprise moments when God met His people face to face, or, declared His own Name and character to them. He is your Shield and very great Reward. He is your Shepherd. He is your "God With Us." He is your Healer. He is your Overcomer. His strength is more than sufficient to fill any of your weaknesses. Only He can fill the holes that leak His peace out of us. Invite Him in and use the chart on the next page to get you started. Close by writing your own Scripture prayers.

Your Peace Robbing Weakness	God's Peace Filling Strength

Write your Scripture prayers here:

_____

_____

_____

_____

_____

_____

_____

_____

_____

_____

_____

Day Four: Peaceful Steps

We learned earlier in our study that the Greek for peace is *eirene*, or "oneness." Being one with God means aligning our perspective with His, aligning our identity with His, and inviting Him into our weakness by confessing the places that, no matter how much we set our mind to it, we just can't get aligned with Him. Being one with God is also asking Him to replace us with Him. Another crucial step to becoming one with Christ is *obedience*.

The first step to obedience is one, up until this point, I've assumed we've all acted on: the obedience of faith that brings salvation. Essentially, this "obedience of faith", as it is referred to in the New Testament, is a simple belief that affects confession and lifestyle. If we believe that Jesus Christ is Lord (meaning the only God) - that we require rescue from our mistakes and sins; that He came to earth, lived a sinless life, and died to pay the debt we owed for our sins; then, He rose on the third day, - that belief will begin a new life in us that leads to verbal confession of Christ and lifestyle changes that reflect the love of God in us. If you have never made a decision to make Jesus your Lord and Savior and want to right now, then turn to the appendix at the back of this study and use that prayer as a springboard to confess your heart to God.

After salvation, there's more life-points for us to get in step with God to cultivate oneness with Him. The Old Testament includes the Ten Commandments and a host of other laws for God's people. Many Christians believe, that these Laws have been fulfilled in Christ, so we can observe them as a way of dedicating ourselves to God, or seeking a life separated from the world. But they are not exactly necessary for God's pleasure or blessing since we are in Christ. An example of this would be in Acts 10:9-11:18. Here the Lord tells Peter to eat things that were banned under the Law and also to share fellowship with Gentiles that would have been excluded under the Law.

In the New Testament however, we are given a set of commands and then a variety of other instructions. Read the following verses and paraphrase them. Then note any life adjustments you need to make based on these directions.

Acts 15:28-29 (the whole chapter is good context)

_____

_____

_____

_____

Romans 12:1-2, 9-21

_____

_____

_____

_____

_____

_____

Ephesians 4:25-32

_____

_____

Ephesians 5:18

_____

_____

1 Thessalonians 4:3

_____

_____

1 Thessalonians 5:18

_____

_____

1 Timothy 2:3-4

_____

_____

John 13:34

_____

_____

By seeking the pathway of obedience in our lives, moment by moment, we practice being positioned more and more in alignment and oneness with Christ. Finally, one last verse: read Romans 14:23 and focus on the last portion of the verse. Paraphrase it here:

_____

_____

The word *sin* means *missing the mark.*[1] In our culture, we often swing between two extremes. For those who have a God-concept, they either dismiss all their spiritual shortcomings and need for salvation by saying, "I'm not a bad person. It's not like I've killed anybody!" Or, we swing to the opposite extreme and think "I can't be close to God because I've messed up so much in my life. I've gotta get cleaned up before I can come to Him."

The truth is, the wages of even the "tiniest" sin, is death (Romans 6:23). However, in Christ and through Christ we can come to the Father freely. As believing, cleansed-from-our-sin Christians, we can now practice obeying the Lord in order to access the privileged closeness to Him Jesus made available to us.

As we choose to not practice obedience, our lives get peace holes and that oneness with Him is weakened - though, thankfully, not destroyed. When we miss the mark by doing anything that is not from faith - even down to eating or drinking, down to that little extra information we shared that slipped the conversation into gossip, or the time we felt out of control in a situation and manipulated someone to make sure things turned out the way we thought was best - all that stuff that doesn't come from believing in God and who He says He is - our peace ruined. Good news though! All of us make peace holes on a regular basis and they can be repaired as quickly as confession from our lips and turning in our heart towards God's ways.

One last verse for you to chew on.

Read and paraphrase James 3:18:

_____

_____

Notice how righteousness (right, in-step-with-God living) and peace are intertwined? Spend some time praying over the peace holes in your life and ask for renewed grace to seek the Lord's pathways in those areas.

_____

_____

_____

_____

_____

_____

_____

_____

_____

_____

_____

_____

Day Five: Peace Under Fire

On all sorts of levels, suffering from a lack of peace in our hearts is an epidemic. We worry, we can't sleep, we pace the floor, we munch, we bite our nails, we drink, we shop, we talk on the phone, we watch psychologists on TV shows to figure life out, we search the internet for answers, we pop pills, and still we crave peace. Anxiety disorders are the number one mental illness in the United States with more than 40 million people being treated annually.[3] Regardless of where we fall on the spectrum of peace-need, its safe to say that not a one of us could say, "I have so much peace in my life I don't have room for more!" While we can admittedly all grow in the cultivation of peace, there is another vital piece of the puzzle we don't want to ignore. The enemy is roaring against God's work of peace in our hearts.

I believe when we mentally and emotionally begin to open the door to fears or worries in our lives, the enemy stands so near that door, he grabs at the peace-fruit quicker than we can figure out what to do about it. As believers, we are possessed by the Holy Spirit. We are God's and God's alone. No one and no thing can have us. However, this wonderful reality doesn't keep the enemy from trying to steal as much from us as possible. He might not be allowed to come in the house, but it doesn't mean he doesn't break the widows and set a vacuum in to try and suck out all the good God is doing in us.

> *Therefore humble yourselves under the mighty hand of God, that He may exalt you at the proper time, **casting all your anxiety on Him**, because He cares for you. Be of sober spirit, be on the alert. Your adversary, the devil, prowls around like a roaring lion, seeking someone to devour. But resist him, firm in your faith, knowing that the same experiences of suffering are being accomplished by your brethren who are in the world. After you have suffered for a little while, the God of all grace, who called you to His eternal glory in Christ, will Himself perfect, confirm, strengthen and establish you. To Him be dominion forever and ever. Amen. 1 Peter 5:6-11 NASB (emphasis added)*

Watch the emotional and spiritual progression in the verse above. If I don't humble myself under God's hand (if I resist the hardships or closed-doors in my circumstances and get angry, prideful and take matters into my own hands), I won't be positioned to cast all my anxiety on my caring Father. I'll carry my own heavy anxieties. This may cause me to be positioned as an easy target for the enemy who is on the prowl. I won't be positioned under the safety of God's hand and therefore I won't be as able to resist the enemy. Most likely I will also be positioned to be slack in my faith and my sufferings will be longer rather than of shorter.

This verse is packed with deep and necessary warnings about the heart attitudes and decisions we make as Christians. We will discuss this verse more in the weeks to come. But attempting to take my anxiety on myself seems to be a doubly weakening move.

First, our anxious burdens weigh us down so we can't journey with God as smoothly or as quickly. And second, they simultaneously seem to add a target to our backs for the enemy to hone in on us. It's like the anxiety baggage we carry has an unbeknownst-to-us red and white bullseye on it; and we sling it on our backs like a backpack for the trek. God help us! What have we done by hanging on to our own worries?!

Like the picture I shared earlier of anger functioning like clearing off a space at a crowded kitchen table for the enemy to sit at and chat a bit, every time the Holy Spirit convicts me of holding on to my worries, in my mind's eye, I see a backpack with this bullseye and I have a choice to hang on or let go. It's hard to let go of our worries. *But how will the bills ever get paid if I don't figure all this out? But Lord, she lied about me and now everyone thinks this about me; how can I just let it go?! But God it's my child, my very heart, and she's in such trouble. But God, how can I just let go when it feels like everything is about to fall apart?*

We can let go only when we see not letting go as more damaging than hanging on.

Satan plays head games and our worries are his specialty. Read the following passages and write a brief summary of each. Note how worry led to disobedience; and how the enemy might have, or did have, something to do with the mess of it all:

1 Samuel 15:24-28

_____

_____

_____

_____

Matthew 26:69-75

_____

_____

Whatever is going on in your life at this moment, the worries aren't worth it. Spend some time journaling your heart to the Lord, casting your anxiety on Him because He cares for you.

_____

_____

_____

_____

_____

_____

_____

_____

_____

_____

_____

_____

_____

Week Five
Cultivating Patience

· ·

Day One
Praying for Patience

Day Two
Our Patient Father

Day Three
His Strength in my Weakness

Day Four
Patience in Action

Day Five
Patience Plundered

Key Verse:
And we desire that each one of you show the same diligence so as to
realize the full assurance of hope until the end, so that you will not be
sluggish, but imitators of those who through faith and patience
inherit the promises. Hebrews 6:11-12

Day One: Praying for Patience

I can remember a Sunday school teacher correcting one of the students saying, "Oh, no, dear. You don't EVER want to pray for patience! Because if you do, God will bring all sorts of difficult things in your life to teach you patience!" It's true that God always answers prayers that are according to His will--including increased patience. But the way I see it, if God wants me to have patience, humility, long-suffering, forgiveness or whatever hard-to-learn quality, it makes more sense for me to pray for it with a willing, desiring heart than to be kicking and screaming the whole time He's teaching me. Plus, if I desire it and pray for it, then maybe the Lord will give me extra grace to make those lessons in patience pass smoother and stick better! So! Are you ready to pray for some patience? Buckle your seat belts, 'cause here we go!

The word for *patience* in the fruit of the Spirit passage is *makrothumia* (mak-roth-oo-mee'-ah). It means forbearance or fortitude, and longsuffering. (Just to tickle you, our culture is so far gone into the depths of the instant-gratification-fast-food way of thinking that longsuffering doesn't even show up in my computer's spellcheck bank! Hopefully, that word is in *our* vocabulary though!) In the New Testament, there's two Greek words which can both be translated as our English word for *patience*. One means *endurance*; it's a kind of patience that bears up under trial or hardship. But the *patience* in our passage is the same one used to describe how we are to wait for the coming of the Lord. "Therefore be patient, brethren, until the coming of the Lord" James 5:7. It means *keep on waiting*! I must confess, I'm a bit glad we're studying the "just wait" version of patience instead of the "keep waiting and waiting under all these hard things" version of patience, aren't you?

Is there something you've been waiting for? What it is?

_____

_____

_____

_____

How do you respond when you have to wait for something? Do you feel frustrated or anxious? Or some other emotion?

_____

_____

What tests your patience the most and why do you think that is?

_____

_____

_____

_____

Different things in life highlight my patience holes at different seasons. There's been some seasons of life where I've been a good girl and had my grown-up-I-can-wait-panties on for our financial needs/issues, for people around me who are going through an ugly phase of growth (you know what I mean?), for goals to be achieved and even for traffic. Then there's times when I don't seem to have patience for any of it! Yikes! I hate being inside my skin when I hit that I'm-totally-out-of-patience wall. The trouble with me hitting that wall is the answer to my patience void is exactly what I don't want any part of at that moment...or that week, or that season. The answer to it is to calm myself down, rest in God's sovereignty and resume peaceful waiting, with a positive, hopeful, smiling Proverbs 31 woman face. Join me for a slight rabbit trail.

My hubby every now and then reminds me gently that the Proverbs 31 woman looks at the future with a smile. I've told him I'm pretty sure the translation for the word *smile* could also be: *she grits her teeth as she hangs on for dear life to this roller coaster that has kidnapped her*. It's not true though. The Hebrew there means *smiling* and in some cases it is translated as *laughing*. As in carefree, cartwheels in a sunny field with Jesus, kind of smiling at the future. Lord, help me!

Back to patience, smiling, peaceful-waiting-patience. Do you ever get impatient with life too? Do you ever feel like your life has become a white-knuckle roller coaster you just can't stand a moment longer? Gosh, I hope I'm not alone! Sometimes I am so done with whatever I am waiting for I just want to go hog-wild and fling myself into excess. Tired of penny pinching? Tired of biting your lip around that coworker? Tired of cleaning up someone else's messes? Tired of juggling work, the house, the degree, the *all* of it? I've been tired of waiting for relationships to come, relationships to heal, relationships to grow. I've prayed for one particular request for nearly 30 years--and that request is entirely in line with God's heart in Scripture--but no movement toward the hoped for answer has come. I will say though, I prayed for one request for ten years and finally when all the odds were against it, the Lord answered the request to the affirmative! But wow! In the meantime, in the dusty, messy, earthy meantime, patience is really hard!

Since patience is such a hard thing for us, have you ever wondered why in the world God wants to develop it in us? Read and paraphrase the verses below:

Ecclesiastes 7:8-9

_____

_____

_____

1 Timothy 1:16

_____

_____

Hebrews 6:11-15

_____

_____

According to Scripture, God's reasoning behind His bent to teach us patience is very much for our good! It's so we won't be foolish and arrogant. It's so our lives can be a witness. It's so we can hang in there and fight the good fight in order to obtain the inheritance of promise and blessing He desires for His children.

Consider the garden of your heart. Is patience blooming? Is there weed chocking it out? Lift up the areas of your heart where irritation, frustration and anger reside. God cares even more about these matters than you because they involve the matter of your growth in Him. Talk it out with Him. Also, write some of today's Scriptures on your 3x5 cards to carry with you through your week.

_____
_____
_____
_____
_____
_____
_____
_____
_____
_____
_____
_____
_____

Day Two: Our Patient Father

Yesterday we learned the meaning for the word patience simply meant, *keep waitin'
sister*! A rather, ordinary, nothing terribly deep or fascinating word meaning--at least
to us. But today we are going to dig into what patience means to our Lord. If there's
anyone who can turn ordinary into extraordinary, it's Him!

When the Bible speaks of God and His patience, it is usually in context with His
being slow to become angry with us. Praise God!

Read Romans 2:4 and note the significance of God's patience toward us.

_____

_____

_____

Can you think of a time when God's patience, or God's patience through another
person, led you to repentance?

_____

_____

_____

_____

Read and paraphrase 1 Peter 3:20:

_____

_____

_____

During the time of Noah, God was so exhausted with the people, Scripture records
that the Lord was sorry He even made man and that He was grieved in His heart
(Genesis 6:6). Despite God's deep disappointment in all of man's wrong and wicked
choices, He was patient and waited for Noah to build the ark before He let the flood
waters envelop the earth. He was patient in order to rescue mankind from total

destruction. God waited to tell Noah to build the ark until Noah was 480; then He waited another 120 years for Noah to finish the ark; then He waited for the animals and Noah's family to get on the ark before He shut the door and released the flood waters of judgement. Even within the stories of God's judgement and wrath there's always strong cords of patience and longsuffering running through it.

His patience does not end with Noah, of course. It continues to this very day as the Lord is patient with even those whom He knows will never come to Him, yet they are all a part of His intricate plan. Read and paraphrase Romans 9:22-23

_____

_____

_____

_____

The vessels of mercy are you and me, while the vessels of wrath are those who will never repent. Yet God, like a master painter, uses the darkness to magnify the light and He is waiting for His plan to be completed in all of His people. And until then, He will wait to pour out His judgement on the earth, just as He did in the days of Noah.

It's this same word for "patience" in the Greek as the word used for the fruit of the Spirit. This is not a character trait of God that He wants to keep to Himself. He wants to replicate it in His children.

Read and paraphrase Exodus 34:6

_____

_____

Has God been patient with you? Has God been slow to anger over something in your life you knew He wanted changed? Write your encounter with God's patience:

_____

_____

_____

Day Three: His Strength in My Weakness

If the Lord wants to replicate patience in His children, and He does, then we must be slow to become angry, just as He is. We must delight in repentance more than justice and compassion and grace more than our personal rights. Reread and paraphrase Exodus 34:6-7, read a few surrounding verses to gather the context of these words.

_____

_____

_____

_____

When you think of God and His personality, is this the God you picture, or do you expect God to be breathing down your neck waiting for you to mess up? Explain.

_____

_____

_____

_____

It's interesting to me that this beautiful declaration of God's patience is in the midst of His giving the Law. We are dust-with-God-breath-inside creatures and we only use less than ten percent of our brains. In fact, the average person uses less than five percent, only super geniuses use ten percent. So we have a hard time wrapping our little bit of usable grey matter around God's standards of holiness, justice and Law while simultaneously wrapping that same bit of brain around His compassion, love, grace and mercy. So we tend to flop from one extreme to the other. We struggle to see God as Love and as Justice at the same moment.

I have a beloved family member who grew up in a church that preached if you sin, you aren't saved-- "saved" is only for "perfect" people. She lived under a crippling sense of guilt and condemnation that stunted her growth in Christ until decades later. Another friend's church journey was filled with esteem boosting messages. She didn't experience guilt. But she also never heard that sin was dangerous. As a teenager, she found herself in some very dangerous sin. God's hand spared her life, but her journey could have cost her life. Years later she deeply regretted this missing peace of obedience in her relationship with God. Now both dear sisters are moving forward in faith, following God, and freedom. Yes, God is Love and yes, God is Holy. He's big enough to wrap His heart and mind around both notions. God wants us holy, He wants us to love like Him, and He wants us to be patient like Him too. Read and paraphrase the following verses:

Psalm 86:5, 15

_____

_____

_____

_____

Psalm 103:8

_____

_____

Psalm 145:8

_____

_____

It's clear God in Scripture that God wants us to understand He is not an angry God and that if we are going to grow in His likeness, we need to let go of our anger and its triggers. The arch enemy to patience in our hearts is our own frustrations, irritability and anger. Our culture teaches us to demands our own rights. Usually, our patience gives way to anger when our rights have been breeched in some way or another.

While anger might be easy to spot in our lives, it is still a God-given emotion. Like sadness, anger isn't a sin, but can be handled in sinful and damaging ways. Anger can motivate people to stand up to injustice. Our bodies respond to the anger in our minds and emotions by supplying chemicals that can give us physical strength to protect, rescue and help in an emergency situation. But more often than not, rather than helping us stand up, it cripples us and our relationships. Like most difficult emotions, anger can act as a warning signal that something in our system isn't aligned right. Pain flags our attention to a physical need; emotions can work the same way by flagging our attention to a heart need.

Dobson cites anger as a more complicated emotion than many of our other feelings. The triggers for anger come from so many different places, including extreme fatigue, embarrassment, frustration, and rejection.[5]

I am far more prone to get snappy when my blood sugar is low. In fact, sometimes my husband or sister just grabs my arm, pulls me away from whatever I'm doing and say, "Go. You need to eat." Then I know I've blown it. Many times it's my tone of voice or facial expression and I'm totally unaware of it--but the person on the receiving end isn't! (Though it is most often my computer, rather than people!) Usually I'm not as bad as it sounds, but, my sister and husband know I would never want to be short or snappy, especially when it wasn't meant to come across that way. One time someone I truly adore was being out-of-character, really hard on someone else at church and it was almost a knee jerk reaction for me to go over there and offer him some nuts and an orange. I didn't though because I realized it might be just a tad too over-bearing. Only those closest to you are allowed to call in a time out!

What's your anger trigger? Is there a time of day you are more susceptible? Is there an activity (competitive sports or something like that) or a relationship that triggers anger?

_____

_____

_____

_____

_____

Sometimes merely thinking through our actions and emotions and having to take note of them helps us become more aware of them and invite the Lord in to change us.

Since there are so many sources of frustration, impatience and anger, it's not as clear-cut to prepare the Scriptures for us to look up and learn to apply to our lives. Maybe defensiveness or fear stirs up a hot temper in you and you need to see the Lord as your Defender. Maybe all the out-of-controlness of life bubbles your frustrations to the surface and you need a perspective shift to see God as Sovereign over everything to calm your heart. Maybe your unforgiveness and wounds revisit your heart strings through anger and you need to release them to the Lord who holds you as the apple of His eyes and will bring justice where it is needed. And possibly, you need to dialogue with the Lord about a physical aliment and seek wisdom to discover pain management. Below are a few verses addressing these anger triggers. If there are others you know of, use a concordance to do your own hunting for God's answer to your patience gap. Write a brief paraphrase of each verse and then use them to fill in the chart below.

The Lord is your Defender

Psalm 18:2

_____

_____

Psalm 27:10

_____

_____

Psalm 61:3-4

_____

_____

Psalm 91:2

_____

_____

Proverbs 18: 10

_____

_____

The Lord is Sovereign

Psalm 46:10

_____

_____

Psalm 100:3

_____

_____

Psalm 138:8

_____

_____

Isaiah 25:1

_____

_____

Isaiah 46:9-10

_____

_____

The Lord Sees your Hurt

Zechariah 2:8

_____

_____

Romans 8:28

_____

_____

Romans 12:17-21

_____

_____

The Lord Sees your Need

Psalm 41:1-3

_____

_____

_____

_____

2 Corinthians 9:8-11

_____

_____

Philippians 4:19

_____

_____

Matthew 9:35-36

_____

_____

Fill in the chart below based on the verses from today's study. I know it was a lot of page turning. I'm praying for all those verses to wash over us and give us a new desire to pursue patience. Dialogue with the Lord over your need to grow in His patience.

Your Patience Robbing Weakness	God's Patience Filling Strength

Day Four: Patience in Action

The Lord often provides perspective and balance for my life through my husband. During one rather dry-on-patience season I was running through my laundry list of intolerant behavior from other people. My sweet man looked at me, took my shoulders and said, "How do you think we'll ever learn in real, practical life to bear with one another unless people feel at least a little difficult?" Oh! He was right!

Years ago, so "ago" it feels another lifetime, we came from a youth group that loved us up one side and down the other to a group that flat out didn't. The Lord had clearly moved us, but I wasn't prepared for them. Children can be brutally honest, and while I adore working with teens, teens have a few more practiced years on them without the veneer adults acquire. Holy Smokes! It was a rough ride! The previous youth pastor had a very different approach to ministry and had also left under some not so happy circumstances. We were worlds apart from what they were accustomed to and they were angry about the situation with the previous youth pastor. The details about the words, the actions and the meanness don't matter anymore and wouldn't bless anyone to repeat. But, I will say there were more than a few nights I rushed outside in the dark of the night behind the youth building and cried. At one point, one of the student leaders had crossed so many lines of kindness and respect, I begged a more seasoned ministry wife for wisdom. She said she would have pulled that student out so fast they wouldn't have known what hit them. And for everything this teen had done and said, it would have been justified. But as my husband and I prayed over it, we felt that even though the whole thing was hard and painful, God wanted us to be examples of grace and humility to them. There was so much arrogance in the midst of that group you could smell it out in the parking lot before you ever got inside. Humility is caught, not taught. So we tried to be gracious and humble the way the Lord is to us. I made food for kids whose parents never had a family meal, and I cleaned up after them, even to the point of them flicking their food on the floor and asking if I was "going to get that." They never said thank you. I gave rides to surly, silent passengers. I took kids to get frozen yogurt after school, only to later hear the only reason they wanted to hang out was they were on restriction and their parents decided I was the only person they were allowed to hang out with--great! I was part of the punishment! I did a lot of things that squeezed my pride. Before all this, I'd had a job. I had a neat, tidy job without food flicking and that made money. Now I was a youth pastor's wife who did, as it'd been described, "the unimportant stuff." Yup. Pride squeezing!

Fast forward about ten years. We still have relationship with some of those kids. Some of them have grown into devoted servants of the Lord. One student even came back not too long ago and told me how much God had humbled her. One of those silent teens apparently appreciated that I always made her feel wanted and loved. I had no idea. Notes and Bible verses we'd sent were saved. Hearts received God's love and truth because they were packaged in tangible grace and patience. His longsuffering leads to repentance in us, and quite often He wants to use us as those vessels of longsuffering for others.

Read and paraphrase James 1:19

_____

_____

_____

Read and paraphrase the following verses. For those of you fellow word lovers out there, these passages contain the exact same Greek word for patience as the fruit of the Spirit passage--no other varieties of patience here!

Ephesians 4:1-3

_____

_____

_____

_____

Colossians 1:10-12

_____

_____

Colossians 3:12-13

_____

_____

_____

2 Timothy 4:2

_____

_____

James 5:10-11

_____

_____

Who is God calling you to be a vessel of patience toward?

_____

_____

_____

_____

Is the Holy Spirit prompting any areas where you might need to repent of impatience?

_____

_____

_____

_____

As we saw in day one, God wants us to have patience because it makes our lives a testimony and opens doors of promised inheritance to us. Patience can be hard because it demands the denial of self, but it's cultivation is worth far more than any thing we could ever hold at it's expense.

Spend some time journaling your thoughts and then make your 3X5 cards with Scriptures from our study so far to help you grow in God's patience.

_____

_____

_____

_____

_____

_____

_____

_____

_____

_____

_____

<u>*Day Five: Patience Plundered*</u>

In day four of week one, I shared how the Lord opened my eyes to the heavy spiritual consequences of anger. God's word has a number of warnings about anger, both as to how it affects us individually, relationally and also spiritually. Read and paraphrase the following verses, personalize them if it's applicable to the verse.

James 1:19-20

_____

_____

_____

_____

Colossians 3:8-10

_____

_____

Ephesians 6:4

_____

_____

Galatians 5:20-21

_____

_____

_____

_____

Matthew 5:21-22

_____

_____

_____

_____

Proverbs 29:8

_____

_____

Proverbs 16:32

_____

_____

Psalm 37:8

_____

_____

Anger in and of itself, for the tiniest of moments, might not be a black and white sin, but it leads so quickly to sin that we must get rid of it! The Lord considers our anger not to be a fleeting emotion, but something weighty inside us. If I only have so much heart space to provide the soil for God's fruitful work, I don't want to spare a patch of it on anger. Not only is anger poison for us as individuals, it also leaves us open to some pretty ugly spiritual consequences too. Sometimes our anger is flash in the pan, extreme forms of irritation or frustration. That kind of anger needs to be processed and brought under God's control. But then there's another type of anger that comes from an old festered wound. Deep anger can also come from envy or jealousy. Did you see the movie *Amadeaus* about the fellow musician contemporary of Mozart? I wasn't crazy about the movie because of all the drama and dark emotion to it. But the movie received great accolades. I wondered if the movie captured so many people's hearts and minds because perhaps that sort of deep envy, jealousy and anger runs through a lot of peoples' hearts and so the plot spoke to that struggle. It's the hot anger that comes from the kind of ambition that will suffer no one to stand in the way of success. It's the anger that comes from giving the enemy a foothold.

Read and paraphrase the following verses:

Ephesians 4:26

_____

_____

James 3:16-18

_____

_____

_____

The James passage will come up again in our study down the road. Jealousy and selfishness can certainly foster anger. And then the topic of peace came up as well. Many of our emotional and spiritual issues are tied to one another, like a tangled vine. That suits the enemy just fine because it makes it so hard for us to untangle our emotional mess that we can despair of ever finding the way out again. Especially when our anger is tied to a relationship, it can be complicated to get things smoothed out and healthy again. Think of how anger affects your marriage or a family relationship or maybe someone at church. Is there selfishness involved or jealousy that blossomed into anger? Did that anger sit overnight? Did the enemy have a field day with it? Yeah. Me too. But there is a way out. In Jesus Christ there is always a way out. Read and personalize this verse below:

1 Corinthians 10:13

_____

_____

James 4:7-8

_____

_____

_____

Nine times out of ten it is best to submit ourselves to a situation because it has been sifted through God's hand (sometimes we do need to put an end to abuses or inappropriate behavior, so don't misunderstand me), to humbly (like get on our knees kind of humbly) draw near to the presence of our God and hide ourselves there so Satan can't disturb us. Always, ever and always, pray that God would make the sin "exit" signs bright and clear in your life. Pray for the Lord to give you the desire, discernment and grace to head toward the escape He provided in this anger-tempting situation. Lastly, there's a few more verses about our relationships to help us guard our hearts against the temptation to become angry. Read and paraphrase the following verses:

Proverbs 14:29

_____

_____

Proverbs 15:1

_____

_____

Proverbs 22:24-25

_____

_____

Proverbs 19:19

_____

_____

Ask the Lord for understanding in a frustrating situation. Ask Him for a soft answer in tone, content and even body language. From my linguistic days in college, I found the difference between the ways men and women communicate very interesting. When men confront one another they often use much softer tones, words, and body language than the average woman (not all the time, but average); they may also say the hardest part of the confrontation while they are not facing or making eye contact with the other man. This scenario might play out as one man keeps talking, but refills his coffee mug or something. Women on the other hand... we are much more demonstrative and emotional in our confrontations. Hence the disconnect we see our men undergo when we start to pour on the passion...angry passion, that is. A soft answer will help the other person not get angry, but it also does something in us. When we refuse to feed our anger it's like putting a lid on a fire and starving the oxygen. We've been taught in our culture to vent our anger. Usually the more energy we pour on our anger, the hotter the flame gets and the farther we get from solving the real problem at hand.

While we need to reign in our hearts, we also need to guard them. Just like certain relationships can be peace robbers, some can also be sticky sources of anger-feeding crazy-making. Remove or limit your involvement with those people. Pray for them, bless them, be wise around them.

_____

_____

_____

_____

_____

_____

Week Six
Cultivating Kindness and Goodness

. . . .

Day One
Kindness and Goodness

Day Two
His Kindness and Goodness

Day Three
His Kindness in Us

Day Four
God's Goodness in Us

Day Five
Kindness and Goodness in Action

Key Verse: Now for this very reason also, applying all diligence, in your faith supply moral excellence, and in your moral excellence, knowledge, and in your knowledge, self-control, and in your self-control, perseverance, and in your perseverance, godliness, and in your godliness, brotherly kindness, and in your brotherly kindness, love. For if these qualities are yours and are increasing, they render you neither useless nor unfruitful in the true knowledge of our Lord Jesus Christ. 2 Peter 1:5-8

Day One: Kindness & Goodness

This week we will study *kindness* and *goodness* together because their meaning in Greek is so close to one another. Interestingly, not only are *kindness* and *goodness* occasionally translated interchangeably with one another, but next week's word for study, *gentleness*, is also sometimes the English rendering for the Greek word in our fruit of the Spirit passage for *kindness*. So, depending on your Bible translation, your fruit of the Spirit list might say "kindness, goodness, gentleness" or it might say "gentleness, goodness, meekness." or it might be a paraphrase and say something different. But, before I get you chasing your tail around trying to understand what these Greek words mean in English, let's get straight to their definitions.

The word for kindness is *chrestotes* (khray-stot'-ace); meaning: usefulness, i.e. moral excellence (in character or demeanor), also translated as *gentleness, good (-ness), kindness*.[1]

The word for goodness is *agathosune* (ag-ath-o-soo'-nay); meaning goodness, i.e. virtue or beneficence. [1]

You can see how it might be hard to distinguish a clear difference in these facets of the fruit of the Spirit when their meanings are so close, and they are occasionally translated interchangeably with one another. *Vine's Expository Dictionary* clears up some of the ambiguity for those of us who don't read Greek fluently:

Trench, following Jerome [two scholars]*, distinguishes between chrestotes and agathosune in that the former describes the kindlier aspects of "goodness," the latter includes also the sterner qualities by which **doing** "good" to others is not necessarily by gentle means. He illustrates the latter by the act of Christ in cleansing the temple, Matt 21:12,13, and in denouncing the scribes and Pharisees; but chrestotes by His dealings with the penitent woman, Luke 7:37-50. Lightfoot* [another scholar] *regards **chrestotes as a kindly disposition towards others; agathosune as a kindly activity on their behalf**.* [2] Ellipses and bold type added.

I hope that makes a little more sense. To get a clearer picture, let's dig into those Bible passages using these particular Greek words (you're on your way to becoming a word scholar yourself!). Read and paraphrase the following verses:

Kindness/Chrestotes

Titus 3:4

_____

_____

Colossians 3:12 (*chrestotes* is the second adjective describing what we ought to "put on")

_____

_____

Ephesians 2:7

_____

_____

Romans 3:12

_____

_____

Chrestotes may have been rendered in a variety of English words, but hopefully you've got a little more of a picture of the work God wants to accomplish in His children's hearts. Write a prayer of invitation for the Lord to move in an area of your life and heart to grow His kindness.

_____

_____

_____

_____

Goodness/Agathosune

Ephesians 5:9

_____

_____

2 Thessalonians 1:11

_____

_____

Romans 15:14

_____

_____

Luke 8:8 (read Luke 8:5-15 for context)

_____

_____

Acts 9:36

_____

_____

Titus 2:5

_____

_____

Write a prayer of invitation for the Lord to move in an area of your life and heart to grow His goodness.

_____

_____

_____

_____

_____

_____

Throughout the week, we will study these traits in the context of our Lord's character, our Christian life, and the weeds and pests that choke out the heart growth of kindness and goodness. As we close today, (I'm not a Greek scholar, but from my personal study and word nerd background) one of the distinguishing factors between kindness and goodness I see based on the *Vine's* description and based on the Scriptures is this: God's kindness is a necessary ingredient in our salvation and His goodness is a necessary ingredient in our sanctification. Kindness is God's character wrapped with a certain softness; it's the tenderness that doesn't "crush a bruised reed" (Isaiah 42:3). Goodness is the part of God's character that prunes us, digs in deep--perhaps more deeply than we find comfortable--so that good will come out of our lives in the season of harvest (Romans 8:28). The same Lord prepares the soil of our hearts, plants His truth and love in us, prunes, retrains, supports, weeds around, waters and protects from the elements and the enemy. The Gardener applies the same love and care with each act, but the plant sure feels different when He pats the seeds in rich, soft soil than when He prunes back the suckers that it was so proud of. If we can learn to trust the One who gently pats the seeds to only ever use those pruning sheers or digging hoe with the same love and tenderness, the garden of our heart will flourish.

Day Two: His Kindness and Goodness

I'm not sure the average Joe (or Josephine, in our case) would use the word *kind* or even *good* to describe God's most prominent character trait--even if Jo was a believer, it's possible that description wouldn't bubble to the surface of her thoughts. As someone serving in ministry, one of the discouraging walls that both my husband and I have found, is that people often feel that if God were truly good, then such-and-such wouldn't have happened so they blame His lack of goodness or trustworthiness for their hurts. Also, many of us believe God's holiness makes Him more critical than kind. Deep down we often feel His eyes fall on us from heaven with disappointment and fault-finding more than with joy, love or delight. His perfection is so much more complete than our notions of perfection that His holiness doesn't work like "ours" does.

When we seek holiness or perfection through our own efforts we become keenly aware of the non-holy things/people around us. Our quest for goodness often gets warped into perfectionism that rails against those nearest us. We project that same expectation of what it means to seek goodness within our limited human context onto our Lord. We expect that since He tells us He is set apart, Holy, and perfect, that He will act like the most extreme perfectionist we've ever known. His perfection, however, is so set apart it doesn't warp Him or take away from His love, compassion, mercy and grace. He can be both 100% kind and 100% perfect without either trait being compromised. Our dusty, little human frames have a much harder time with this concept.

Read the following verses and personalize each one:

Titus 3:4-7

_____

_____

_____

_____

Romans 2:4

_____

_____

Ephesians 2:7-8

_____

_____

Matthew 11:30 (the word *easy* is our Greek word for *kind*)

_____

_____

Meditate over these verses for a few moments and write your experience of the kindness of God. If you have not personally tasted His kindness, ask Him to reveal Himself in this way to you. If you need a fresh experience of His kindness, ask Him for that as well.

_____

_____

_____

_____

_____

_____

I am praying for you right now, sister, that God's kindness and goodness would fall afresh on you (and me too). We cannot cultivate the fruit of the Spirit in our hearts without being rooted completely in Christ. The development of His fruit in our lives is a direct result of our being wrapped in Him and experientially knowing His love, joy, peace, patience, kindness, goodness, etc.

Read and personalize the following verses describing God's goodness toward you:

Matthew 7:11

_____

_____

2 Thessalonians 1:11-12

_____

_____

2 Thessalonians 2:16

_____

_____

James 1:17

_____

_____

James 3:17

_____

_____

How have you experienced God's good wisdom in your life?

_____

_____

_____

_____

How have you received His good gifts?

_____

_____

_____

_____

_____

_____

Sometimes the simple act of remembering and writing down our past experiences with God can draw us closer to Him for the journey today and keep us closer to Him for the path tomorrow. It is His heart for us to remember Him. The book of Deuteronomy was the only Scripture Jesus quoted from when Satan tempted Him in the desert. Of all the books in the Bible, Deuteronomy uses the word "remember" most. The book that rings in with the second highest usage of the phrase "remember" is Psalms--the book that is said to be the "heart of God" while Proverbs is the "mind of God" book. That little rabbit trail was just to illustrate how very near to God's heart it is that His children might remember Him. Meditate over these verses for a few moments and write your experience of God's goodness. If you have not personally tasted His goodness, ask Him to reveal Himself in this way to you. If you need a fresh experience of His goodness, ask Him for that as well.

_____

_____

_____

_____

_____

_____

_____

Day Three: His Kindness in Us

As we've studied each facet of the fruit of the Spirit, we've also looked for the heart stuff that sits in opposition to each fruitful trait. Some of the opposite traits might overlap. For instance, joy and peace could both be chocked out by the same emotional weed. But for the sake of throughly checking our hearts for those weeds and vines that quench God's work, we've selected one opposite trait for each facet of the fruit of the Spirit. These "weeds" aren't precise or directly from Scripture, but they are based off the Scriptures.

Yesterday, as we read through the passages describing God's kindness, I saw over and over how His kindness spread over my weakness and inability. His yoke is easy; His kindness calls over the shouting of my sin and failing, beckoning me to His embrace; over and above my ability/inability to perform, His kindness speaks louder and stronger. In a tidy package, His kindness stands in opposition to criticalness. A critical eye looks for weakness to pounce on it. His eyes only look for weakness to infuse strength in the need. One of the definitions for *chrestotes* was usefulness. A truly kind heart sees how it can be useful in light of someone else's need, while an un-*chrestotes* heart sees need and decides how to use that weakness for her own gain.

In my personal life, I can attest to the fact that criticalness has been a kindness choking issue. We'll discuss our criticalness triggers later on today, but for now, without blame or self-justification, let's consider our own criticalness.

How has a critical eye or critical words impacted your:

- Relationships

_____

_____

_____

_____

- Conversations

_____

_____

- Ministry to family, friends and church

_____

_____

_____

_____

If it is God's kindness that leads us to repentance, we can bank on the fact that kindness is a key element to our witness. As we consider our daily interaction with family members, co-workers, church family, neighbors, friends and even the people at check-out stands and restaurants--do they see God's kindness spilling out of us, just as He spilled it over us?

Based on the context of God's kindness toward us in Scripture and the Greek definition (moral excellence, usefulness and goodness), I see kindness at work especially when weakness is present in someone else. Kindness is a reaction to weakness. It's a response that protects, covers (in a healthy way, of course) and supports needs or weakness. The opposite response takes advantage of weakness in one of two ways (depending on your personality). Criticalness is perhaps the most readily visible negative response to someone else's weakness. The other response is manipulation. Both criticalness and manipulation play upon the weakness of others. Criticalness uses someone else's weakness to puff up their own ego and feel better about themselves in their own estimation or in the eyes of others. Manipulation attaches to someone's weakness and uses it to get something they need or want from it.

Criticalness is easier to spot in our lives. Manipulation a little harder. It's more sly and sneaky. Read these few passages and then paraphrase each one:

Galatians 5:15-16

_____

_____

_____

_____

Galatians 5:26

_____

_____

1 Timothy 6:3-5

_____

_____

_____

_____

Colossians 3:8-10

_____

_____

_____

_____

Is there an area where you've perhaps allowed criticalness or manipulation to take up heart-space where God's kindness could be cultivated?

_____

_____

_____

_____

Woman relationship dynamics are tricky. We ladies are good at being "nice." Funny how the word nice isn't mentioned in the fruit of the Spirit passage. Funny how someone can be "nice" as she listens sympathetically and with such concern as we spill our guts, our hurting, broken guts, only to hear next week she shared our secret pain as a "prayer request" with all the other women at church. Now the other women can all shake their pious heads at us. Our weakness preyed upon, rather than prayed over. We're good at saying "bless her heart" when we really mean "get a load of this..." Yeah. "Nice" isn't necessarily kind or loving or gracious. But it sure smiles pretty. It can manipulate us and then stomp critical over us in two seconds flat. Kindness doesn't play like that.

Growing up I watched a lot of unhealthy relationship dynamics among the women I very much loved and looked up to. While I was in a college girls' Bible study, we went through a study about friendships. Seemed basic enough. I didn't figure I'd walk away with all that much. But those unhealthy dynamics I'd always taken for granted were called into the light of truth and I began to see how much untangling my expectations needed. Here's some of the thoughts that study prompted.

Healthy Friendship says:
If you need me, I'll be there to the best of my ability. You can count on me to love you without judgement and pray for you through whatever comes your way.

Manipulative Friendship says:
I'm here to be your rescuer - I know you couldn't manage anything without me to pull you through.

Healthy Friendship says:
If you messed up, you need to do what you can to own up to it and make things right. I'll stick by your side as you go through this because I love you.

Manipulative Friendship says:
I will always cover for you. You don't have to take responsibility for what you've done. (Or "I expect you to cover for me. I shouldn't have to take responsibility for my issues. You're always to blame.")

Healthy Friendship says:
I love you, want the best for you and am happy for you when you share sweet times of friendship with other people.

Manipulative Friendship says:
I am your only friend. You can't have any other friends beside me - and everyone needs to know that I am your only friend.

Healthy Friendship says:
It's fun when we like the same things! What joy to share life with you!

Manipulative Friendship says:
You have to like what I like. (Or "I have to like what you like.") We can't have individuality. We have to only like the same things.

Unhealthy friendships aren't built on the basis of trust, respect or Biblical love. They serve the purpose of self. Real friendships will help you grow (Proverbs 27:17), spur you on to love God and His people more (Hebrews 10:24) and they will portray sacrifice (John 15:12).

This kind of manipulation in friendships has no part with moral excellence or looking out for someone else's good.

Without slipping from healthy self-awareness into blame-shifting, take a few moments to consider your personal triggers and temptations for criticalness or manipulations. While you are considering yours, I'll rat myself out first. I get wildly critical when someone else gets critical, especially of someone else.... especially of my family or friends. I come out like Momma Bear when someone is critical of my loved ones. While another person's words might have been my trigger, I can't blame them for the ways I've gotten my own hands completely muddy and often gotten stuck in that mud far longer and deeper than the individual who triggered my poor reaction. I've shredded people beyond reasonability and to the detriment of the person I was originally wishing to protect. It's ugly. And I'm always so regretful afterwards. As a kid, my dad would tell me "It's not your job to set her/him/them straight." As an adult my heavenly Father has repeated those words into the ears of my heart. It's my job to love, show kindness and grace to them, not set them straight. No matter how much I think they are wrong.

Manipulation is one the Lord and I journeyed through long ago. But the temptation to manipulate rears it's nasty little head when I'm hurt and really want someone to see something the same way I do. It's been a long time since I gave into the temptation, but I know I'm not above it. As a minister's wife I think people have a strong sensitivity to being guilt-tripped into church involvement and attendance. I'm careful to (hopefully) not come across this way. When I've worried someone thought my "I missed you last week" was manipulative, I follow up with "and not in the guilt-trippy way, just genuinely missed YOU!" For our lives to be useful witnesses, criticalness and manipulation can't have ground to grow in our hearts. Now, take some time to really consider the soil of your heart and confess any areas that need weeding.

_____

_____

Write the Scriptures from yesterday and today that describe God's kindness and ask Him to fill your kindness holes with the riches of His kindness in you:

Your Kindness Holes	God's Kindness Filling Strength

Day Four: God's Goodness in Us

I think sometimes we ladies have a hard time seeing our un-goodness. One woman I spoke with gave me such a clear picture of this in action. We might not reflect the stark reality of this issue like this sister, but we are wise to ask God for truth in our hearts and humility to swallow the reality of our need before Him. I share this story only because I could see truth in her situation for all of us. One day after a communion service, this sister said she always felt bad after taking communion because she really didn't sin and so she would lie to God and make up sins during the self-reflection and confession portion of the service. Another woman who was part of the conversation said, "Oh! Gosh I don't have any trouble finding things to confess! I can't go a day without being selfish or prideful in the secret places of my heart, if not committing some outward, blatant sin against someone else!" The first woman listened and then held tight to her conviction that she just doesn't sin except to lie about her lack of sins during Communion. Time and life moved us from church fellowship with one another, but I still loosely kept in touch with her. She'd joined a leadership team at her church and was very thrilled with her position. She kept a variety of rules in order to be part of the leadership. She was quite proud of the hardship of her sacrifice. She didn't read her fantasy books, but also didn't regularly read her Bible, and as an older, single adult, played a bit faster and looser than was wise. And still, she didn't have sin to confess. She also was very vocal about God's voice speaking to her about sin in other people's lives. She felt in the marrow of her bones that she maintained a goodness all of her own. She's not alone in this. You see we all far too easily make up our own standards of "good" and create our own personal brownie point system.

We bake 250 cookies for the bake sale, work in the nursery, volunteer at the soup kitchen every month, donate our clothing to the women's shelter, raise money for the crisis pregnancy center, juggle work, home and family and decide all that makes us pretty good people. But we might have done it while we grumbled heavily about it; compared our labors to all the other lazy people who don't do anything--or perhaps we think it's a good thing they don't touch our territory because they could never do it as good as us; we might have juggled all our efforts while flirting with some guy in the office, at our kids' school or even at church...shall I go on? Maybe we just gave and gave but didn't see how our pride snuck in and smeared itself all ugly-like on our very best efforts, turning even our offering to the Lord into dirty rags.

No one sets out to be wrong. Probably 99% of all that we say and do has already been through our personal justification processor. It takes so much grace for us to even see our shortcomings! I often hear unbelievers say they will make it to heaven because they are "good" people. Their standard for "good" is that they haven't killed anybody.

Read and note seven things God takes issue with...they are so "un-good" that God actually hates them!

Proverbs 6:16-19

1. _____

2. _____

3. _____

4. _____

5. _____

6. _____

7. _____

So yes, killing people was in there, but so was being divisive, arrogant, lying lips, planning against someone (manipulation perhaps?) and ogling after bad things happening to someone else.

Within even our sweetest of Christian sister fellowship, we aren't beyond becoming fertile ground for some of these issues. There's times I felt so hurt over something I wanted someone else to see my point, share my pain and ultimately take my side--that equals divisiveness. Who can claim freedom from arrogance? While some of us might not struggle with out-and-out lying, we might struggle to find ways to be completely honest about why we can't attend a social event, or why we just can't eat one more bite of so-and-so's potluck dish. Perhaps, our honesty is tested when we are tempted to exaggerate a story for effect. These "little" things fall short of good in us. They are weeds that choke out God's goodness in us.

While all of these un-good things in us choke out God's good work in us, there's a specific emotion that I think blocks God working good through us into the lives of others. It's jealousy. Think about it. Besides unforgiveness locked in our hearts, what other emotion blocks our desire to see good come on someone else's life? Jealousy and envy want all the good for ourselves. Jealousy and envy can prompt a great many of those qualities from the list of the seven things God hates, can't they?

Now jealousy is one of those ugly things that good Christian girls just "don't" have in their hearts. It's hard for us to admit when we've been jealous. It's too dirty to look at, let alone own up to. We know we aren't supposed to be jealous. We know we're supposed to be all content and joyful in what God has given us. We know we're supposed to rejoice with those who rejoice and not begrudge someone else what God has given them. We know it and that's probably what makes us hate it that we can't just will the ugly emotion of jealousy out of the soil of our souls.

Some years back I was convicted over a sneaky form of jealousy that had rooted deep in my heart. It looked more like discontentment than what I would have termed "jealousy." But I felt the Lord press His finger on it and show me I was jealous. And who or what was I jealous of? Something and someone nebulous. I wanted what "other" young women seemed to have, the freedoms, friendships, the fun, I wanted the general way they lived. I didn't want to take it from anyone, so I thought I was free and clear to indulge my heart in its pining and discontent. "Everyone" else had this, that and 'tother thing. I didn't. I even wished I "had a ministry" like my other friends. That seemed like a perfectly "holy" whine. I'd always defined jealousy as wanting something someone else had--like coveting. But if we defined jealousy as wanting something we don't have because we've seen someone else with it, then we might see our hearts in a whole new light.

If something tickles that "want" space in our heart and we are motivated toward something other than god-likeness, whatever name we slap on that response (jealousy, discontentment, greed, competition) we don't want to feed and fertilize it. I'd been really good at fertilizing it. Now, I will add that God can give us a discontentment that spurs us on toward His purposes, passions and likeness. Maybe we see someone whose passion for Jesus urges us on to know Him more, settle into the world less and seek Him in prayer and in His word. Then, I'd say that's a holy discontentment. And I've been ever so thankful for the men and women God has used in my life to stoke the flames in my heart to love God more brightly and fervently. But just like anger, discontentment is an emotion which mostly does not accomplish the righteousness of God.

For me, this discontentment that became a form of what we'll call "Joneses Jealousy" (from the phrase *keeping up with the Joneses*) let a lot of fruit robbing into my life. It robbed my joy and it robbed my desire to do or see good for others. I wouldn't have articulated it that way, but truth be told, I was so wrapped up in my woe-is-me perspective I couldn't see what others needed. I wasn't available for God to pour His goodness through because I was all wrapped up in my issues. How lame! How sad! How very, very easy!

In high school one of the most wonderful things that happened to me was an incident that left me a bit friendless. It's a long story, that's not for our time, but it was my senior year and my lunchtime was painfully wide open. I knew God had a purpose for it so I walked the campus and prayed for Him to show me who I was supposed to reach out to. Goths were pretty new then and there was a handful of sad looking freshmen covered in black and safety pins. Maybe them? No. I walked some more. Was I supposed to help a teacher? No. Then I saw them. The year earlier our campus opened to severely handicapped children. Most of them lived at Children's Hospital when they weren't at school. Honestly, they were scary. They shouted and made anguished noises. They were disfigured and deformed. They were completely off my radar screen. And it was them I felt the Lord nudge me toward. I offered to help feed the kids because the teachers and aids needed extra hands. It was a messy business, but I began to see the beauty in them. One of the students became my special "buddy" but a number of them I came to know well. I stayed after school and helped more than just at lunch. I found more joy with those students than I could have ever imagined. God was able to pour His good through me because I was available. Specifically when it has come to relationships, there's been more times I sat around moping because I didn't have the friends I pined for or I was up jumping through hoops trying to keep or get friends. This time I embraced what God put before me and that allowed good to pour through.

Whether our jealousy is directed toward a certain person or object, or it's that nebulous discontent or competition, it robs us from having lives positioned for God's goodness.

Read and paraphrase the following verses:

Matthew 27:17-18

_____

_____

Mark 10:15-16

_____

_____

Genesis 4:4-8

_____

_____

Philippians 1:15

_____

_____

Jealousy can lead us to do some pretty awful things. It can even get twisted up in our service to God. For years I'd never really known what it meant to serve out of envy and strife--I just didn't see it. Since then I've come to see it more than I wanted to. One time I was listening to someone who was beginning a speaking ministry. We were praying for the Lord's direction over both our lives and sharing our passion for women's ministry when she said something I'll never forget. She said it was such a great feeling making people want more. I agreed and said I pray God would make me a good salt shaker, pouring salt over people's lives to make them thirsty for more of Him. She kind of gave a start and said, "NO! That's not what I meant at all! I meant want more of ME! I love making them thirsty for more of me!" If we are ever serving and want people to want us, we're too much in the middle of it.

God pours out His goodness without strings attached. Read and paraphrase the following verses:

Matthew 5:43-48

_____

_____

_____

Luke 6:35

_____

_____

Psalm 145:9, 16

_____

_____

Here's a few more verses of God's character:

Psalm 86:5

_____

_____

Psalm 84:11

_____

_____

Psalm 73:28

_____

_____

Psalm 31:19

_____

_____

Psalm 27:13

_____

_____

Psalm 23:6

_____

_____

As we've rambled over the territory of good and not-so-good, is there any heart space that needs weeding and tending from the Gardener? Do you have any un-good triggers you need God's grace infused into? Spend some moments confessing your failings and weakness and then fill in the My Weakness/His Strength chart.

May God's goodness fill you deeply and pour out of your life richly, my sister!

Your Goodness Holes	God's Goodness Filling Strength

<u>*Day Five: Kindness Goodness in obedience*</u>

Well sisters! We've got an oodle to cover today! Without a lot of introduction, let's jump in. Our focus for today is two fold. First we will study direct instruction for how God wants kindness and goodness to pour out of our lives and secondly we will address the issue of the enemy's plan to rob this harvest from our hearts.

Read and personalize the following verses:

Philippians 2:14-16

_____

_____

_____

Mark 9:49-50

_____

_____

Luke 6:35

_____

_____

1 Corinthians 15:33-34 (the word "good" here is actually *chrestotes*)

_____

_____

Ephesians 4:32

_____

_____

Romans 11:22

_____

_____

Colossians 3:12-13

_____

_____

1 Timothy 3:11

_____

_____

Whew! That was a list! God's direction for kindness and goodness in our lives. Write the names of three people you feel the Lord wants to pour His goodness and kindness through you onto them:

1. _____

2. _____

3. _____

Pray a blessing over each one of them

_____

_____

_____

_____

_____

_____

Now, as we wrap up our kindness/goodness study, we have to consider the enemy's plan to steal God's harvest in our lives. Paul tells us we are not to be unaware of his schemes (2 Corinthians 2:11), so read and paraphrase the following verses that tie the enemy to issues of jealousy and criticalness:

James 3:14-16

_____

_____

_____

1 John 3:12

_____

_____

Revelation 12:10

_____

_____

Job 1:9

_____

_____

Psalm 52:2

_____

_____

The accuser is Satan. The name Satan means *accuser*. While there's a great many verses about judgmental attitudes in Scripture, it is safe to say that I want no part of my life to reflect the enemy. While we are called to discern, we aren't called to criticalness. The line might be fuzzy, so I pray wisdom for you and me to lean into the Holy Spirit and know the difference between the two. Envy and jealousy lead to every evil thing, including the first murder. We read earlier the people even handed Jesus over for crucifixion because of their envy. Envy, jealousy, greed, competition, and criticalness are dangerous, foot-hold-giving attitudes in our heart. We are wise to pray actively against these issues in our hearts. Like anger, they can fester and become gaping wounds.

Spend some time asking for God's protection over any vulnerable areas in your heart and denounce any cherished criticalness or jealousy tucked in your soul.

_____

_____

_____

_____

_____

_____

_____

_____

For I am confident of this very thing, that He who began a good work in you will perfect it until the day of Christ Jesus. Philippians 1:6-7

Week Seven
Cultivating Gentleness

. . . .

Day One
The Fruit of Power

Day Two
The God of Gentleness

Day Three
His Strength in My Weakness

Day Four
Walking in Gentleness

Day Five
Humility Promises

Key Verse:
"Take My yoke upon you and learn from Me, for I am gentle and humble in heart, and you will find rest for your souls." Matthew 11:29

Day One: The Fruit of Power

Every time I've tried to imagine the face of Jesus I see love written all over it. But with every gesture and facial expression, I also imagine Him radiating with gentleness. For so many women to have found Jesus approachable in Bible times, when women and men lived in very different spectrums, must have meant He had a gentle countenance, don't you think? For children to have wanted to be near Him, they must have seen Him as a picture of gentleness.

A gentle spirit is rare and hard to find, but what a treasure it is. The Greek word for gentleness is *prautes* (prah-oo'tace). It describes humility. In English such words as meek, mild, humble, and the like have a touch of weakness attached to them. But this Greek word for gentleness has no relation to any weakness.

According to *Vine's Expository Dictionary*, the meekness or gentleness "manifested by the Lord and commended to the believer is the *fruit of power* (emphasis added)." Vine's definition goes on to describe gentleness as something more than just an adjective to describe a word or deed; it's an attitude of the heart before God and men that spills out into all aspects of living.

Prautes is translated in English as a few different words (kindness, meekness, etc.), including gentleness. In English the word for gentleness carries its own meaning. The definition includes: "not harsh or violent"..."docile," "tamed" but goes on to say that it can refer to the status of a person, such as nobility. Hence, we have the word gentry. (I do believe I am starting to sound like Gus from *My Big Fat Greek Wedding*, but hang with me here!) The very meaning of the word gentle gives us insight into what our Lord wants for us. He is calling us to power and strength that is displayed through a refined, (elegant if you will) regal and quiet spirit.

Gentleness "is the fruit of power" bestowed on us by God. I once heard meekness described as a Clydesdale horse that had been well trained. The horse held within him the power to stomp or kick anyone near him into oblivion, but he allowed trainers to lead and care for him. When we practice humility and gentleness, we are not weak, rather we are strong.

The *Vine's* definition includes another important aspect to our word *prautes - selflessness*. "Meekness is the opposite to self-assertiveness and self-interest; it is neither elated nor cast down, simply because it is not occupied with self at all." A humble heart is not concerned with itself. It neither asserts its own rights nor does it walk around with its head hanging low.

Does this definition differ from what you thought it meant to be humble? If so, explain how and then think of someone that exemplifies humility to you. Write the practical ways you've witnessed him/her display humility.

_____

_____

_____

_____

Self-centeredness can take on many forms. The gal who pops in front of the mirror every hour to check her hair and make-up might be self-centered. But the girl who is all wrapped up in Eeyore-style - "I'm not worth fixing up," "No one even looks at me anyway," "Can't do much with this hair anyway, why bother" - is also pretty self-centered because she is constantly dwelling on herself! Both are centered on self; one for one reason and the other for another reason. It's all the same in the end.

Is there an area where your self-focus needs to be altered? Write it here:

_____

_____

_____

I had a string of events where someone kept saying things about me that weren't true. The slander sat right down on some old-wound heart space that just shouldn't have been sat on; but then again, the Enemy (not the person, but in terms of our spiritual battle) never plays fair. As I wrestled with this nagging upset over who all was getting an ear-full, what should I do or not do about it, and how could I ever continue a relationship with this person who just wouldn't stop lying about me, but whom I loved very much, the Lord spoke some hard words over my soul. I felt like He showed me it was my preoccupation with self that worried what other people thought. It was self-absorption that held me bound to the pain of this situation. If I gave up caring, I could give up the pain. Of course relationship adjustments (sadly, hard ones in this case) have to be made in a circumstance like this. But ultimately, I had a choice to make as to how deeply I would let this vex me.

Read and paraphrase Galatians 4:6

_____

_____

This passage tells us that we are sons (and daughters) of God and that we have an inheritance from our Father. The inheritance Christ received was incredible glory after breath-taking sacrifice. This is the interesting part of the English definition for gentleness I mentioned earlier. While the word denotes a docile or tamed heart, it is also tied to the word *gentry*, signifying nobility, wealth, and honor. This is a beautiful picture of our Lord who subjected Himself to the lowliness and even the worst cruelty of humanity, but was given all glory in His resurrection. This too is our inheritance. However, our hardship is so trite compared to that of our Lord's. Yet displaying His Spirit of humility and gentleness is our calling - sometimes a rather daily and difficult calling - as the requirements of pouring selfless humility out for others can feel like emotionally or spiritually washing stinky feet.

Ungentle tendencies erupt in different forms in each person and personality. For some of us, our self-centeredness causes our pride to be easily offended. For others it means that we demand to be on center stage. Others are sarcastic and cutting in their attempts to "up" another individual. And then there's all the easy absorption in "my" goals, "my" priorities, "my" agenda, "my" precious schedule, etc. "Me" and "mine" can easily take up so much room that there's little left for Jesus and others. Look into your heart and pray over where your ungentle tendencies grow. Ask the Lord to uproot them. Read and paraphrase one last verse, James 1:21.

_____

_____

_____

The truth will set us free. But it is only through humility that we're able to receive the Word into the soil of our hearts. Ask God for humility. Ask Him to show you where it's lacking.

_____

_____

<u>*Day Two: The God of Gentleness*</u>

Part of defining each facet of the fruit of the Spirit is understanding that trait within the context of the Character of God. I don't know about you, but there's been more times than I can count that I thought I was doing something loving or peacemaking or kind, only to find out my actions were in one way or another shortsighted. As we continue our study of gentleness today, we will dive into the gentle Character of Christ.

Read and personalize each of the following verses:

Matthew 11:28-30

_____

_____

_____

Matthew 21:5

_____

_____

Isaiah 40:11

_____

_____

1 Kings 19:1-19

_____

_____

_____

_____

Our God is a gentle God. As we wrestle against the wild earthquakes and fires of life, trying our best to serve Him and keep our heads above water, we must always remember that He is gentle. He is not a demanding task master, but a Master with a light and easy burden. It's the rest of the world that rages harsh against our souls, not our Father.

The meekness of our Lord is something that, for me, is hard to grasp firmly enough to hold in focus in my memory. I mean consider the all powerful Creator King of the universe and everything that exists beyond the boundaries of our discovery, putting the hallmark of His image on one creature: man. And those two set-apart-ones (man and woman) disobey Him. The only creatures to bear His image turn against Him, publicly, before all the rest of Creation. And in that moment, God did not send lightening from His throne to strike them down in the very place they stood. No, He came to find them, to talk with them, to provide a covering for their shame and a promise for healing. That is gentle. When He came to fulfill that promise made at the Fall, He emptied Himself, not only bearing our sins, but bearing them through poverty, rejection, lowliness, injustice, unfairness, and in genuineness. If I had His choice, I might die for the world, knowing I'd rise again, but I wouldn't endure birth and potty training, childhood teasing, adolescent insecurities, acne and awkwardness, young adult pressures, the needs of a real, flesh and blood man, and then the real pain of the cross. He emptied Himself of every right, privilege, and power that could have shielded Him from His own rejection and pain. He did all this because He wanted us to see and know Him.

So often we ascribe to God the character traits of the harsh fires and storms in life, when He isn't in them. When we do that we make Him out to be someone other than who He is. Read and personalize these verses:

Psalm 56:8

_____

_____

Matthew 10:29-31

_____

_____

Psalm 116:1-2

_____

_____

Deuteronomy 4:31

_____

_____

Genesis 16:13

_____

_____

Isaiah 30:18

_____

_____

John 13:5

_____

_____

Our Lord has caught every lonely, broken tear you've ever shed. He counts the hairs on your precious head. God compassionately watches over your life to inject His graciousness. Jesus is the God who bends down to hear your prayers and wash the dirt from the soles of your weary feet.

Some of us have personally experienced the gracious, gentleness of God. If you have, write your experiences in the space provided on the next page. If not write a prayer asking God to reveal this part of Himself to you.

Day Three: His Strength in my Weakness

On the journey from hole-y to holy, we continue our search for the Spirit leaks in our soul, confessing them and asking God to fill them with His strength.

We have to become aware of the places and ways we lack gentleness or humility. I once heard (and for the life of me can't find the source!) about an old Christian classics author who labored over a manifesto of what it means to be humble. As the words spilled masterfully and eloquently on his much prayed over pages, he felt the twinge of satisfaction...self satisfaction... and he was so very proud of how well he had captured and communicated the essence of humility. Then he saw it. His pride! Frustrated, he crumpled it up and tossed it in the garbage. Yes, true humility is most elusive to us.

Most of us don't set out to be arrogant or prideful. We make it our aim to be humble. But our hearts are so tricky, we hide our pride from our own eyes. Read the following verses and write a prayer after each one for the Lord to open your eyes to the truth in each verse:

Proverbs 8:13

_____

_____

Proverbs 11:2

_____

_____

Proverbs 29:13

_____

_____

Mark 7:22

_____

_____

Romans 8:1-3

_____

_____

_____

1 John 2:16

_____

_____

As you prayed through that set of verses, was there a person or circumstance that came back to your mind more than once?

_____

_____

_____

_____

_____

You might try asking someone close to you, who loves you enough to be honest, to tell you when or how you lack humility and gentleness.

Years ago, when I first started in full-time ministry, I was coordinating VBS. It was at the end of the week and I was tired. I was the bottom rung on the office totem pole and all sorts of people were ruffled all week long about the impact the outreach made on the church space. I'd managed adults old enough to be my parent or grandparent who'd never participated in a VBS before. Though eager, they were unexperienced, like me. There'd been surprising mishaps (like kids bringing knives to the VBS and threatening other children...and then having the guardian come and threaten me). There'd been oodles more kids than we planned on and all week we scrounged for food and supplies (good problem). Suffice it to say, by the close of the week, I was beat!

Our pastor always wanted lots of pictures of every event and insisted that everyone in attendance be assembled and photographed. Then there was the "workers" photo that came at the very tail end of the event with everyone who'd lent a hand. It was a beautiful thought, but wasn't always that easy to pull off. The church wasn't much for altar calls, and we'd had one at the close of VBS with a really wonderful number of children and even parents come forward. For many of those involved, it was their first time experiencing this sort of event (altar calls weren't typical for this particular church) and the Lord reaching through all of us in that amazing way He does. They were all chattering with joy and excitement. But I was tired.

My smile jar was empty. I'd worked to keep adults humming along in organization, fixed problems, used all my techniques to keep our oodle of kids focused and directed, and now the adults were refusing to listen...when I was SO tired! I snapped at them. *Do ya think you could just pay attention long enough for me to get one little picture?! Geez you're worse than the kids!* They were surprised and then quickly posed for the picture. As I wrapped up the final messes before I could go home and collapse, my husband looked at me and said, "You should never speak to people like that. Especially your elders who have helped you so much. You were too harsh. You didn't have the right to speak to them that way."

He was right. Painfully right. I stammered about how he could see they weren't listening and he just repeated, "It wasn't right."

When Jesus came in all His gentle grace, He didn't snap at people when He was tired or hungry. He didn't demand His way or His rights. He laid them down. We all know it and ascent to follow it mentally; but emotionally it's a much harder path to follow. It's a dying path. A crucified path. An impossible-for-us-without-Him path.

Look back over all the verses we've studied together on God's gentleness and pray them into your ungentle holes. May God grace us enough to be honest before Him and ourselves about this heart-space within us.

Your Gentleness Holes	God's Gentleness-Filling Strength

Close with this last precious word: Psalm 18:35. Blessings, dear sister as you press into the gentle heart of our Father.

_____

_____

_____

_____

_____

_____

_____

_____

_____

_____

_____

_____

_____

_____

_____

_____

_____

_____

Day Four: Walking in Gentleness

At every moment of the day we have the opportunity to think, feel, or speak arrogantly, or humbly and gently, towards whatever or whoever is in front of us. On the road, in the grocery store, in your too-crowded bathroom at home when everyone needs in at once; in the privacy of your thoughts when your husband is late again. At every conversation juncture there's a opportunity to be gentle or self-absorbed. Even in the way we listen to one another we can be gentle. Couldn't you use a gentle ear when your heart is in need.

A dear couple struggled under the weight of a health issue. Eric and I met them for prayer. We tried to listen to their hearts. We'd heard of a possible treatment for this health ailment and shared it with them; but we also said we didn't want to tread in their private business. The husband said, "We are just so tired of everyone telling us what to do to fix it." They were bleeding out their eyeballs with this faith-stretching, soul-searing hurt. Everyone's quick-fix remedies felt like a slight to their pain. No one meant it that way. The couple was in shock, just trying to make it through a day and weren't really addressing treatment because they were so overwhelmed and uncertain of what to do next. All of us outside their shoes just wanted to help. But our ears weren't always as gentle as they could have been; and our best intentions spilled out a bit arrogantly from our mouths. This only added to the very hurt we were all trying to pray away. Gentle ears are able to hear the soul-cry of those around us, beyond just the words their lips make. Gentle-eyes are able to see needs that self-absorbed ones never could. Lack of humility is so very stealthy, even in our best intentions.

All my best intentions, no matter how good they were meant to be, amount to one thing, a pile of *me* and *my*. And *me* and *my* aren't Jesus.

Read and paraphrase Isaiah 64:6

_____

_____

Our struggle to not be continually moving in self and to move in God's gentleness is monumental and impossible without the Holy Spirit. Gentleness is described in Vine's as "the fruit of power." When we walk in Christ's gentleness, our pride and flesh may be crushed a bit, but they're really only pressed under the weight of God's glory coming down to spill out and over our face-to-the-ground, humbled lives.

Read and personalize the following verses:

1 Peter 2:18

_____

_____

Ephesians 4:1-3

_____

_____

_____

Colossians 3:12-14

_____

_____

_____

Titus 2:3:1-2

_____

_____

_____

1 Timothy 6:11 (read a few surrounding verses for context)

_____

_____

Most of us would say we want more of God's power infused into our hearts. The verses in today's lesson are the power socket; our obedience is plugging into that power. As we soak in the verses above, the instruction for gentleness is a general approach to life. These next verses are more specific life situations. They apply gentleness or humility instruction to very specific areas. Read each verse, paraphrase it, and pray through this area in your life:

In your heart

1 Peter 3:3-4 (if you want, you can go on a side trip and read Isaiah 3:16-18)

_____

_____

In your witness

Philippians 4:5

_____

_____

1 Peter 3:13-16

_____

_____

_____

In your ministry/service to others

1 Timothy 2:24-26

_____

_____

Galatians 6:1

_____

_____

In your wisdom

James 3:13

_____

_____

Romans 12:6

_____

_____

In your words

Proverbs 15:1

_____

_____

Pray through your heart-garden's harvest of gentleness. Spend some time writing Bible verses from our study on your 3X5 cards. I am praying God's grace for both of us, that at each crossroad of gentleness or pride, we might have the eyes to see the path God is calling us to; and that our feet would follow Him deeper and deeper into His gentleness of Spirit.

_____

_____

Day Five: Humility Promises

Most of us love the promises of the Bible. They sit out on the horizon of our lives, like a golden sunset, beckoning us forward in obedience and faith. Most of the time. Sometimes, we like to cherry pick our promises a bit. Those golden sunset ones are there for the purpose of feeding our faith. The other "promises" or warnings are there to hedge us away from the wrong path. Those hedgy promises are the ones we usually aren't so keen on memorizing and taping on our bathroom mirror. Today, we've got a mixture of the two...

Read and personalize the following verses:

Matthew 5:5

_____

_____

Psalm 25:9

_____

_____

Isaiah 57:15

_____

_____

Proverbs 11:2

_____

_____

Proverbs 29:23

_____

_____

James 4:10

_____

_____

1 Peter 5:6

_____

_____

A heart of humility can rest in a place of God centered confidence because the Lord promises to protect us when we are tucked under His hand, humbly waiting on His timing and plan. It can feel lonely, dark, crushing, and a myriad of other things we don't like when we humble ourselves and allow God to handle a difficult situation instead of handling it ourselves (or just squawking loudly about it as we go). However, under His hand is the safest place for us to be.

A heart that makes room for pride can also have confidence in the consequences that come after pride. Read and paraphrase each of the following verses:

Proverbs 16:18

_____

_____

Isaiah 2:11-12

_____

_____

Ezekiel 28:17 describes the Enemy how? (You can read more of the chapter for context, but hone in on that verse)

_____

_____

1 Peter 5:5-10

_____

_____

_____

_____

James 4:6-7

_____

_____

Satan's downfall was his pride. We are warned throughout Scripture that pride sets us up for a fall. And in 1 Peter and James we see the Enemy lurking too close to those verses that warn us of pride and exhort us to seek humility. Pride comes so easily and costs us so dearly. It was the moment Eve decided that her perspective was clearer than God's that she bit into pride; and then into the fruit of consequence. God help Eve's daughters to surrender our deep roots of pride in our hearts! May the vision of God's promises for the humble set clearly on your horizon today. Write your heart, Scripture prayers, or any other responses to the Lord:

_____

_____

_____

_____

Week Eight
Cultivating Faithfulness

· ·

Day One
Filled With Faithfulness

Day Two
The Faithful One

Day Three
His Faithfulness In My Weakness

Day Four
Faith in Action

Day Five
The Enemy Of Our Faith

Key Verse:
I pray that the eyes of your heart may be enlightened, so that you will know what is the hope of His calling, what are the riches of glory of His inheritance in the saints and what is the surpassing greatness of His power toward us who believe. Ephesians 1:18-19

<u>*Day One: Filled With Faithfulness*</u>

It wasn't until I dug into the word meanings of the Fruit of the Spirit passage that I realized what sort of fruit "faithfulness" was truly meant to be. I figured it meant loyalty. And since other attributes pertaining to relationship are mentioned in the list, it seemed natural that loyalty would be among them. However the word in Greek is *pistis*, meaning "firm persuasion," and "conviction."[1] It is *belief.*

Faith is a small and simple word that gets tossed around our world rather easily. "Keep the faith" is our local baseball team's slogan. "Have a little faith" is often a phrase meant to encourage. In my high school we had a "faith" club instead of a "Christian" club. Somehow the word "faith" was less offensive than "Christian," even though it was just a Christian group. No matter how we treat this word, living it out is an entirely different matter.

Read and paraphrase the verses below and consider how faith is not only foundational for our journey with God, but it is also the framing, the windows, the plumbing, the electrical, and the roof!

Ephesians 2:8-9

_____

_____

Hebrews 11:6

_____

_____

Ephesians 6:16

_____

_____

Matthew 15:28

_____

_____

Galatians 3:22-29

_____

_____

_____

_____

Ephesians 3:12

_____

_____

Take a moment and consider how the faith in your heart is flourishing. I remember at a retreat years ago I confessed the sin of unbelief. I labored in prayer over it and loathed it so much I was sure I would step forward afresh into a journey hence forth free of that nasty, ugly unbelief. I told the woman discipling me about my resolve. She said that was a good place to be, but that I might find more unbelief tucked in heart-corners in the future. I was sure she couldn't be right. She was. Well, sort of. That unbelief wasn't just tucked in heart corners out of sight. It was sitting right down in the middle of my heart's living room. It danced in my mind and played it's music so loud I couldn't hear anything else. Tucked in the corners? It was in a whole lot more of my heart-space than I could have realized.

We are quite capable of gathering around a campfire fire and singing happy faith songs. We quite easily hang signs in our houses that say "Faith," wear jewelry or sport bumper stickers that say "Faith;" but the reality of our unbelief could (and I write this with so much love!) be having more of an impact in our daily lives than our faith does.

In our Western world, church life (meaning you and me and all of us professing belief in Christ) has become characterized by what has become known as "practical atheism." We live our lives mostly disconnected from God, except for Sundays. We may slip in a mid-week Bible study if we're really zealous (or, when we are in a jam). We don't need God to put food on our table, heal our baby's sickness because medicine isn't available, or a host of other daily needs. We just sort of need God to make us feel better when life gets hard. And when He doesn't do it fast enough, we turn elsewhere. Even when our soul is crying for His nearness, our feet are walking further and further from His presence. I've been guilty of this. And in my wandering, when the thorns and thistles of life surrounded me, my unbelief shouted things like:

- "Why did God do this to me?"
- "God must not love me or He would have protected me from this!"
- "If this is what I can expect from a so-called loving God, what's the point?"

Unbelief shouts and shouts into the echoing emptiness of soul that it produces in us. Unbelief was our foundational brokenness and faith is our foundation for healing. Read Genesis 3:1-8 and describe the process and fruit of unbelief:

_____

_____

_____

_____

_____

_____

_____

Unbelief produces a broken relationship with God. Notice how God still spoke with His children, provided for them, and interacted with them. As believers, we can have access to God through our belief in Christ, yet fall short in our belief in so many other ways. He will still provide for us, speak to us, and interact with us, but our relationship will suffer for our unbelief. Unbelief brought an openness to hear and heed the voice of the enemy for Adam and Eve. It brought disobedience and arrogance toward God's instruction. It brought separation between husband and wife. It brought shame and hiding from God and each other. Unbelief is very costly.

Spend a few moments in prayer over your faith; and over the presence of unbelief in your heart. Through prayer, make room for the beautiful things God wants to do in and through your precious heart.

Day Two: The Faithful One

Unlike Eve who was plopped into paradise, many of us were shaped by painful or dark experiences before we really even had a chance to develop enough mental maturity to understand faith in God, or to understand His Character. I was blessed to grow up in church, but painful early childhood experiences clouded my view of God. I believed in Him and even believed He was who He said He was. But I believed He'd only show up for certain people. For those precious in His sight He would be strong, He would protect, He would part Red Seas and close lions' mouths. But I was sure that I wasn't among those worthy enough for Him to rouse Himself from His high and lofty throne to take notice of me or my circumstances.

So for me, He didn't feel all that trustworthy. I would worship Him for being good since I had read that He was good and had heard that He was in other people's lives; I figured He's God and should be praised. I had much to be thankful for and counted those things as His gifts to me. But I didn't personally taste His as much of His goodness as was actually wrapped around my life. My taste buds were too coated over with the bitterness of pain to taste much of anything else.

I know I'm not alone in this. Our circumstances can leave such an awful taste in our mouths that we don't even know how to "taste and see that the Lord is good (Psalm 34:8)." So we take our disappointments and pain into the depths of our souls. And because we can't understand how God figures into all this, without flatly declaring how we feel He has mislead us or not been good to us - (heaven forbid...transparency like that would make us bad church girls, right?) - we just shut God out. We build walls of unbelief around our hearts so we won't be disappointed again. And we quiet the sobbing of our souls by burying all of this under steely unbelief.

As a younger Christian, I remember reading Romans 5:5 and wondering what in the world that verse was talking about. It says, *"And hope does not disappoint, because the love of God has been poured out within our hearts through the Holy Spirit who was given to us."* I believed the Bible was true, but could not imagine how Paul could make the claim that hope wouldn't disappoint us. Maybe *his* hope didn't disappoint him, but mine had. I knew Christians close to me who had been broken in their deep disappointments. It has been years of wrestling this faith thing out, being disappointed, being hopeful, laboring in prayer and seeking wisdom, that has helped me come to a place where I think I understand better the kind of faith God wants to grow in me; and in you.

You see, faith is so often thought of as something we put more in an outcome than in a Person. We seem to think that faith is something that will get us through to the other side of a hard circumstance and on to greener pastures. If we just have enough faith, then we will have what we want. It's easy to arrive at that conclusion. For starters, we'd like it to be that easy. Under this belief system, if we could just mount up enough faith, then we'd have more control over life, less disappointment, less pain.

James 5:15 says, *"and the prayer offered in faith will restore the one who is sick, and the Lord will raise him up..."* Now, we could study the context of this verse and find that it possibly refers to sin-sickness more than a physical sickness. We could discuss the usage of the Greek word "sickness" in the passage. But let's put that aside, since most of us in this study believe that God can and does heal physical illness. And if we've held this belief for any length of time, we also have seen fervent, faith-filled prayer offered for those who were not healed of their sickness on this earth. And so we wrestle. Maybe it wasn't God's will. Maybe our faith wasn't good enough. I've heard people believe that someone had sin in their life and God turned His ear from our prayer. Maybe we should have fasted more. Many of us writhe with our wrestling under these questions.

As I've stared down personal disappointments over family pain, ministry pain, relatives taken with cancer, our journey with infertility, etc., I've come to realize God isn't looking for me to have faith in a greener, other side. I don't need to have faith in the circumstances improving; in fact that might possibly even be flat-out wrong. I need my eyes fixed simply and completely on Jesus. I need faith that is rooted in His goodness, His love, His trustworthiness, His provision - Him alone. I don't need faith in the people around me (no matter how much I love them), or faith that one day we'll have a child, or that one day all my family pain will be replaced by sunshine, or that one day things will get financially easier, or that one day things won't be so hard. I just need faith that says, God is with me. God is greater than my circumstances. God is Sovereign and loving and good. Yes, God parts Red Seas and changes water into wine. Yes! He does reach into our lives and say "with Me, nothing is impossible." Yes. But whatever He changes, touches, heals, or does is just a reflection of Him. It is not the goal of our faith--He is.

Have you ever put your faith in a circumstance instead of in Christ alone? When and what was the outcome?

_____

_____

_____

_____

_____

Have you been resting your faith in God or in the "greener, other-side"? Explain.

_____

_____

_____

_____

Read over these next verses and jot down your response to each one:

Daniel 3:15-18

_____

_____

_____

_____

Esther 4:15-16

_____

_____

Luke 22:41-44

_____

_____

_____

_____

1 Corinthians 10:13

_____

_____

_____

_____

Hebrews 11

_____

_____

_____

_____

_____

_____

_____

_____

Faith is costly, but so is our unbelief. When we look at our circumstances, we will find disappointment. But like those who have walked strong in the Lord before us, if we reckon that we are strangers in this world and welcome the promise of God "from a distance" there will still be wildernesses, temptations, affliction, and ill-treatment; but there will also be walls that fall down, battles won, healing, and the promise of heaven. Even Jesus' earthly journey involved sweating blood to walk in God's will (see Luke 22:43-44). We will be immensely disappointed if our faith rests in getting our way or our comfort in this life. The only safe place to rest our faith is on God alone.

As I sought to trust God's Character more than God's handiwork in my circumstances I came back to this verse over and over again. Read and personalize 2 Timothy 2:13:

_____

_____

_____

_____

Even when we get fixated on our circumstances and shake our nasty unbelief at God; or hide our hearts from Him under it, He is still faithful to us! Praise Him! He is now and forever our Faithful One!

Read and personalize the following verses:

Revelation 3:14

_____

_____

Revelation 19:11-16

_____

_____

_____

_____

1 John 1:9

_____

_____

Hebrews 10:23

_____

_____

1 Thessalonians 5:24

_____

_____

Write a prayer of thanksgiving for all God's faithfulness over you. Have a testimony of His faithfulness ready on your lips. Some one might need it someday!

_____

_____

_____

_____

_____

_____

_____

_____

_____

_____

Day Three: His Faithfulness In My Weakness

Many Christians look at the Old Testament and think that it was a covenant of hardline rules and that the New Testament is an obedience-loose, grace-without-expectations zone. I think we get that notion from a quick read of the text without deeply soaking in the words Jesus left us with. He said in the Sermon on the Mount that lusting after a woman was just as bad as committing adultery with her; that anger toward another was just as bad as killing them; and that while the Old Testament allowed for revenge, following Christ means turning the other cheek, walking an extra mile, loving and blessing those who persecute us. Tall order, big expectations. Another passage like these is found in Romans 14:23. Read and paraphrase the verse here:

_____

_____

_____

This verse calls us to consider our motives and worldview. If we operate in anything less than faith, we are sinning. Yikes! Fears, unbelief, doubts all need to be dealt with and processed with God so they don't override our motivations. Do we make plans in faith or fear? Do we serve as wives in faith or fear? Do we parent in faith or fear? Do we tend our finances in faith or fear? Do we have friendships rooted in faith or fear? Do we fulfill our work obligations in faith or fear? The last time we argued with our spouse or children, was something other than faith involved in the emotions we felt?

Write your thoughts and ask God to illuminate places in your heart where something less than faith drives you:

_____

_____

_____

_____

_____

_____

160

This concept is so all consuming! Our fears are so sneaky and our circumstances often cement those fears deep into our hearts. Read and paraphrase or personalize the following verses:

Genesis 15:1

_____

_____

Exodus 14:13-14

_____

_____

Joshua 1:7-9

_____

_____

1 Chronicles 28:20

_____

_____

2 Chronicles 20:15

_____

_____

2 Chronicles 32:7

_____

_____

Isaiah 51:7-8

_____

_____

Matthew 10:28-31

_____

_____

1 John 4:4

_____

_____

As you soak in those passages and consider how God is calling you to a deeper, higher, and wider faith, commit yourself to His grace and ask Him to fill your lack of faith with His faithfulness.

Read Mark 9:24 and make it your own prayer:

_____

_____

_____

_____

Fill out the chart on the next page just as you have the previous weeks:

Your Faith Holes	God's Faithfulness

I so very much hope you are blessed by this exercise. It has been a blessing to me! I pray God's faithfulness to be so loud in your life that it drowns out the noise of everything else!

Day Four: Faith in Action

Today we've got so much to cover I want us to jump right into our Bible study! Read and paraphrase the following verses:

Hebrews 6:11-12

_____

_____

Ephesians 1:18-19

_____

_____

_____

Faith in God's Character, His Word, and His promises accesses His power and brings His promises into our practical reality. The territory that covers where we are today and the spiritual ground we wish we lived in (more abundant peace, full joy, sweet humility, others-centered love, enduring patience, etc) is joined by a road of faith.

In our previous days of study we briefly studied the importance of placing our faith in Christ alone, rather than putting it in people, things, or circumstances. This study on faith is so short; we really haven't done it adequate justice. I hope this has wet your appetite to dive deeper into your own personal study of the Character traits of God. While our faith in God's Character is of the utmost importance to our faith-journey, there is a second important facet of our faith (which some of my favorite Christian authors have written on). It is believing what God says about us and our identity in Him. Our belief in what God says about Himself is critical; but so is our faith in what He says about us.

If I believe the thoughts that run through my head about my worth, or cling to the sharp words of others to reflect my value, I am 100% less likely to experience an adventure of faith in my life. I'm going to trust my God less because, well, how can I trust Someone who obviously flubbed so much when He created me. If I believe the song the world sings about what is valuable, beautiful, important or desired, I'll be so stuck in my short-comings my vision of God will be precluded by my short-sighted and self-centered focus. Believing that I am God's chosen child, beloved, clean, freed, a victorious conqueror, frees me from all the self-image baggage I've collected along the way. I mean seriously, if we could see all of our self-image baggage like luggage at the air port, imagine all the suitcases and the places-we've-been stickers we'd all have gathered. When I believe God is who He says He is, and that as my Creator I am defined by Him alone....wow. Everything changes in my perspective.

The burdens we carry through life get so much lighter when we dump that self-image baggage and trade it in for the identity Christ holds out to us. And "faith" is the conveyor belt we put all that baggage on. Turn to the appendix and read the *Who I am in Christ* list. Then write the ones that convicted your heart or touched you the most here:

_____

_____

_____

_____

_____

_____

_____

How does believing what God says about you free you up to follow hard after Him?

_____

_____

_____

_____

_____

_____

Faith cleanses our identity and frees us to move forward in the journey God has for us. In a message given by Bruce Wilkinson, he said he believed miracles covered the territory between the place where I live according to my ability and the destination where God wants me to be. That destination demands more than I could ever give; its a place of total dependence. It's a place we get to by asking "What does God want done here?" instead of asking "What can I do here?" (Those great questions belong to Mr. Wilkinson.) Believing what God has to say about His Character and believing Him for our identity allows us to run the race, instead of constantly tripping over ourselves or our mistrust of God; getting side tracked, or finding a puddle in the sidelines to sit in. Believing God's Word over our life means the kind of stuff found in the following verses. Personalize each one:

2 Peter 1:3-5

_____

_____

_____

_____

2 Corinthians 12:9

_____

_____

Romans 8:32

_____

_____

1 Thessalonians 5:24

_____

_____

Psalm 138:8

_____

_____

Hebrews 12:2

_____

_____

So we've established that unbelief costs a lot; and our faith is also costly. It was given to us at great cost and it will require cross-bearing sacrifice from us. We've also touched on two places that specifically cultivate faith: in our view of God's Character; and in our view of our own identity. There's two more points I want to address in our study today (told ya we had a lot to cover!).

How do we grow our faith? The answer: we desire to grow in the Lord. As we've hashed and rehashed, our growth depends on God's grace, but involves our response to His grace, truth, and love. Sometimes we unknowingly hold on to stuff that weighs us down in our journey. Sometimes we know we're holding onto to stuff, but we just don't know how to let go. Like all the other facets of the Fruit of the Spirit we need to ask God for a sensitivity to the opposing issue in our heart--in this case unbelief. We need to be sensitive to unbelief in our thoughts, in our emotions, and motives. Then we need to confess and repent when we've surrendered that faith-space to unbelief. After repentance, we ask for God's strength to fill that place of weakness. Hence the chart we've filled out every week. It's a rinse-and-repeat sort of process. While this process is the same for all the Fruit of the Spirit we've studied, faith has a unique element to it's cultivation. Read and paraphrase Romans 10:17:

_____

_____

It is absolutely imperative to our growth that we are personally devoted to the absorption of God's word. If we want to have a growing faith, then we need reading eyes, a listening heart, and lives that readily conform to the design and direction found in the Bible. When we studied the cultivation of love in our lives and viewed bitterness as the opposing heart issue, we saw an interesting spiritual reality. The

Book of Hebrews warns us to make sure no bitter root springs up among us so that no one would miss the grace of God (Hebrews 12:15). It's the only time we learn about a way we can "miss the grace of God." Choosing to hold onto bitterness means our grace receptors are blocked by the bitterness we hold. When we reject the Word, either through simply not reading it, or if we read it, we don't let it change us, our faith receptors are blocked as well. It's a self-feeding cycle. The more we read/expose our hearts and minds to the Word, the more we want to get the Bible in us.

Faith in action in our lives means we believe what God says about His character, our identity, and we actively wash our minds in His Word to prepare the soil of our hearts for the cultivation of deeper and broader faith. Lastly, we need to know how God wants us to live faith out in our everyday lives. Read and apply these verses to your own life right:

Matthew 25:14-40

_____

_____

_____

_____

2 Corinthians 5:7

_____

_____

We've read Hebrews 11 earlier, but skim back over it and consider the life context of each "hall of faith-er." Was it in their personal life or public life that these great feats of faith were carried out?

_____

_____

_____

_____

All my life I've looked up to people in ministry who did really great things. Missionaries, servants through whom God moved hundreds and thousands to repentance, you know...the amazing ones. While Scripture does indeed tell us that quality servants/pastors are worthy of double honor, I think we tend to elevate their service in our minds to the point of the discounting of the service God has entrusted to us. It's as if we believe that what Billy Graham has to say is really important because it reaches thousands of people, but what I say to the gas station clerk or my neighbor isn't as important because it's just one individual. Untrue. In God's sight, that little note of encouragement to a friend in need is just as valuable as a Christian best-seller. Your prayer for a sister in private is just as sacred as a revival meeting message in public. The conversation you had with that precious eight year-old in Sunday School is just as worthy and valued as the ministry the "big wigs" fulfill. Be faithful in what God has placed in front of you. The private, personal struggles and needs are part of your sacred, faith cultivating journey. There is no piece of your life too insignificant to not become a vital part of the tapestry of God that He is weaving in your life and in the life of His Church as a whole.

Spend a few moments in prayer asking God for direction and conviction as to how He wants you to pursue living faith out in your life:

_____

_____

_____

_____

_____

_____

_____

_____

_____

Day Five: The Enemy Of Our Faith

Scripture doesn't come out and precisely say what the Enemy wants to steal from us most. But if I had to guess, I'd say it is our faith. We know that he is a thief and a liar (John 10:10, John 8:44). So in regards to our faith, he will always be throwing lies our way about the nature of God, hoping to cause our eyes to lose focus on Christ, so that we remain fixated on the lie he just flung in our path.

Read Job 2:4-5 and paraphrase what kind of response Satan was hoping to provoke in Job:

_____

_____

_____

_____

Satan wants us to see God's character as warped and flawed; and, for lack of a better term, curse-able. Little wonder as to why he would set this as priority number one in his attack-strategy when we consider the following verses:

1 Peter 5:8-9

_____

_____

_____

Ephesians 6:16

_____

_____

Luke 22:31-32

_____

_____

_____

2 Timothy 4:7

_____

_____

1 John 5:4-5

_____

_____

_____

If Satan can damage our faith, deceive us into lowering our shield with disappointment or disillusionment, he can quite simply hamstring the rest of our following after Jesus with very little effort.

Take the rest of your devotional time today to pray God's protection and strength into your faith. Use the Scriptures we've covered this week to write on your 3x5 cards.

Be strong and let your heart take courage, all you who hope in the Lord. Psalm 31:24

Week Nine
Cultivating Self-Control

· ·

Day One
Engaging Your Self-Control Muscle

Day Two
His Control

Day Three
Called to Self-Control

Day Four
Self-Control in Action

Day Five
The Enemy of Our Self-Control

Key Verse:
But since we belong to the day, let us be self-controlled, putting on faith and love as a breastplate, and the hope of salvation as a helmet. 1 Thessalonians 5:8 NIV

Day One: Engaging the Self-Control Muscle

My hubby bought me a game for my birthday. I love games (insert big smile). He got me this game called Blokus. I've been obsessed. I think I burned out the rest of the family on it. The game is a little like tetris, only instead of trying to fit the blocks tightly together, you fit them tightly and connect the four different colors of blocks by corners only, no same colored sides touching. I just really want to fit all the pieces on the board! And the internet says its possible, so I'm determined. So far no success. You can play it with up to four people, or play it like solitaire. And since everyone else seems to have less of an urgency about fitting all these plastic pieces on the board, I've been playing it by myself. The other night Eric and Mandy were telling me to put the thing AWAY as I told them how I just really *needed* to make them all fit. Eric looked at me and said, "sweetie...self-control!"

Some years back we had a student in youth ministry that was full of energy. One night he'd been listening to the lesson but when he couldn't sit still for one more second, walked across the room and began having a conversation with one of the other students about some action figure. Eric was unflustered, despite the unusual interruption. "Dude, self-control. Just a little bit longer. Self-control." He said it graciously, but gave this student the answer to the situation. Just apply a little self-control and we'll all get through this!

A Christian family I've watched on TV decided self-control was so important to teach their children that they began instilling the value of the trait in their toddler years. They actually had a "self-control" exercise for the little ones. It consisted of quiet time while Mommy read to the bigger kids. The wee one had a blanket s/he could crawl around on (but not beyond the border of the blanket) and just one special toy to play with. The only time they could play with the toy was on the quiet time blanket. Kids are bombarded with venues for instant gratification... EVERYONE in our culture is bombarded with instant gratification opportunities.

We have become desensitized to the value of self-control, as if it isn't important to us because there's always some way out of needing it. It's almost as if *self-control* is just a word you'd expect to hear the grandma in an old black-and-white moving saying with a wagging finger. It's just so out of date for our culture. Since self-control seems irrelevant to us, we miss cultivating it and then when we wish we could engage it, we come up lacking.

I love that self-control is the finale of the fruit of the Spirit list. We can't love without self-control; we can't have joy without self-control because that instant gratification need robs us of joy; peace and patience are fertilized when self-control is flourishing in our hearts, and so on. Self-control is foundational to our spiritual growth.

Of all the fruit of the Spirit qualities, it's the one I wish I'd been taught to cultivate before I reached adolescence. Can you imagine if you already knew how to apply self-control to the intensity of hormone changes, mood swings, girl drama, boy drama and life-shaping decisions that accompany life from 12 to 20? Teaching children to value self-control is a great gift. And it's one I think we pass on through example. Self-control is a vital part of our legacy as well as a very important way we glorify God in our lives.

The word self-control used in the Galatians passage is *enkrateia* from *kratos*, meaning: strength and mastery.[1] *Vine's Expository Dictionary* explains the necessity for self-control like this: the various powers bestowed by God upon man are capable of abuse; the right use demands the controlling power of the will under the operation of the Spirit of God.[2] Exercising a spirit of self-control will undoubtedly bring out the best of the gifts and talents God has entrusted to you. Self-control is denying our self-indulgence or self-centeredness to make a conduit for God's strength to flow freely in and through our life. When we yield to the Holy Spirit we are making room for His strength and mastery to enter our heart, mind, and relationships.

List a few things in your life you know would grow and develop with the application of self-control:

_____

_____

_____

_____

_____

_____

As we've studied how each fruit of the Spirit facet can be derailed by an unhealthy emotion, self-control is ultimately the stop-gap we apply in the cultivation of God's strength in our weakness. Before we allow a thought or emotion to take residence in our valuable heart space, we take it before the Word and the Holy Spirit to see if it lines up with the fruit God wants to cultivate in our lives. If it doesn't we, deny it access to our heart, mind and life. If you're like me, this is a messy process that is usually much slower that I wish it was.

Read and paraphrase the following verses:

2 Peter 1:5-8

_____

_____

_____

_____

1 Corinthians 9:25-27

_____

_____

Proverbs 6:23

_____

_____

Proverbs 12:1

_____

_____

Proverbs 23:12

_____

_____

Hebrews 12:11

_____

_____

Self-control involves our yielding to the purpose and power of God in our lives. It also means receiving His discipline and being self-disciplined. Spend some time considering the areas of life God wants to grow self-control in you. Perhaps ask a relative or someone close to you where they think you would benefit growing self-control. Write it down, be honest with yourself and get prayer accountability from a sister.

_____

_____

_____

_____

_____

_____

_____

_____

_____

_____

Day Two: His Control

While God desires to grow self-control in us, it's not a concept foreign to His character. He is the essence of self-control, despite His being perfect and not requiring self-control to overcome sin the same way we do. As Jesus walked our dusty terrain, He regularly engaged in self-control, self-discipline or some other form of setting Himself aside.

Read and note Jesus example in the following verses:

Matthew 3:41-52

_____

_____

_____

_____

Matthew 4:4-11

_____

_____

_____

_____

John 6:38

_____

_____

Philippians 2:5-8

_____

_____

1 Peter 2:21-3:2

_____

_____

_____

_____

Toward His earthly parents and His heavenly Father, Jesus showed submission and set Himself aside so that God the Father could use His life for the purposes and glory according to the design.

List a few of the ways God has called you in the past week to yield yourself to His purposes:

_____

_____

_____

_____

_____

We ladies can be great at setting ourselves half-way to the side. We set ourselves aside just enough to do the job, but hang on to enough of ourselves to grumble while we work or we do the service but with strings attached. It's hard for us to set ourselves completely aside and let God flow freely through us to feed, tend and love His lambs.

Is there an area of your life where you sense the Lord calling you to deeper self-control? Is there an instance in the recent past where you perhaps did the half-way thing where the service was given, but tainted with self-centeredness? Yesterday we read a few verses that spoke about receiving discipline. Is there an area of life where you've perhaps resisted the discipline of the Lord? What area of life is God tugging at for you to yield control or focus to Him?

Write your thoughts here:

_____

_____

_____

_____

_____

_____

_____

Fill out the chart on the following page, just like we've done all the other weeks, use verses from our study to fill in God's strength and lift up, confess and repent of the places you have self-control holes.

Your Control Holes	God's Strength of Power

In closing, read Colossians 1:29 and make it a prayer. Use the Scriptures from our study thus far to pray the Lord's control into the areas of your life that need greater submission to His power and purpose:

_____

_____

_____

_____

_____

_____

_____

_____

_____

_____

_____

_____

_____

_____

_____

_____

_____

<u>*Day Three: Called to Self-Control*</u>

Recently I saw a word-art piece on pinterest that said: *Creativity is messy. I am very creative*. Are you creative, too? I am....very (wink, wink)!

When we were first married and I read a ton of books to get direction on how to manage a home--a point at which I entered marriage nearly cluelessly. I read a variety of organizational books. This one gal had her calendar planned out six months in advance (filled) by the hour. Her calendar was as sacred as holy water and no one dare inconvenience it. This was apparently the *only* way to maintain order in life. And that also apparently meant I had no hope for organization...ever! We've always had people pop in unexpectedly, need us at a moment's notice, add things, change things and just pretty much monkey with every plan or schedule we've ever made. Nothing sacred about our calendar! You too?

It seems as though the principle of flexibility was often more important to fruitfully serving than rigid self-disciple. In more recent days, I sense the Lord calling me to learn the skill of maintaing both concepts in more mature balance.

Sometimes life is like learning to drive a car. At first just steering, keeping the gas steady and breaks smooth takes all our concentration. Eventually we are able to drive, have an intelligent conversation and perhaps listen to music too. Sometimes just learning to manage one task is all we can really wrap our heads around at the moment. But eventually, our focus will be able to, and need to, stretch around other facets of life as well. I've personally found my self-control "muscle" works this same way. I focus on cultivating self-control in one area, but eventually God calls me to grow it in another area. That new growth becomes a bit all consuming and then after a while, things flow smooth and steady, until of course, He moves me on to the next area.

With all the demands life places on us, it's easy to allow those pressures to influence our prayer and Bible study habits more than the Holy Spirit. It's easy to allow tiredness to dictate how much energy we pour into our relationships with husbands, children, family, or church. It's easy to lapse out of healthy exercise or eating habits when we have financial crunches or some other consuming focus.

Whether we need self-control to quit a habitual sin or to simply manage life with greater faithfulness to God's glory, the good news is that we have access to the self-control we need!

Read and personalize the following verses:

2 Timothy 1:7

_____

_____

1 Corinthians 2:16

_____

_____

2 Corinthians 5:17

_____

_____

1 Thessalonians 5:8

_____

_____

Of all the fruit of the Spirit facets, I think I am most glad to stop and consider that the old is gone and I am new in Christ with regards to self-control. Even when I've slipped into self-indulgence, been lazy and the pile of untended laundry heaps and flows (or whatever it is that has runaway with life) where discipline and order should be, that verse beckons me forward. The day we turn to Christ for salvation we are made new creatures, but praise Him, the work is on-going. So everyday that promise is fresh for us. New depths of "newness" await us. We are never called to sit in the pile of "old" just because we've made a great big mess out of our lives. We are always called out of our sin and weakness to new depths and heights of strength.

If our minds need a thorough cleaning or healing, we can grab hold of the mind of Christ as our own. I don't understand the mystery of this verse in it's fullness. But there have been times in my personal journey when life tested my mental stamina and I hid myself in that verse. Moments when stresses or sadness sat down so hard on me my mind bent a bit under their weight and I prayed, "Lord I can't fathom having *Your* mind, but grant me access to it now. Cover my mind in yours. Let me into your sanctuary. I rest in the promise that I have the mind of Christ here and now."

Our self-control doesn't rest in our ability. It rests on Christ in us and us simply yielding to His Spirit within us. Isn't that good? It's cause for praise for this girl! Spend some time praising the Lord for His ability, strength and control in your life.

_____

_____

_____

_____

_____

_____

_____

_____

_____

_____

_____

_____

_____

Day Four: Self-control in Action

Putting self-control into action can take on many different forms. If you are married, it might mean you spend time in prayer pouring your heart out to God and allowing the Holy Spirit to help you process some heated emotion before you let your upset charge full blast at your spouse. It might mean making a commitment with some accountability to not discipline your children when you're angry. If you are living under your parents' roof, it might mean going the extra mile to ensure relationship success with your parents and family. Exercising self-control boils down to knowing when and how to deny our impulses for the purpose of making way for God's strength to flow freely in, through and out of us.

Read the following verses and paraphrase some of the contexts in which we need self-control:

1 Corinthians 3:7-9

_____

_____

_____

_____

1 Corinthians 9:23-27

_____

_____

1 Timothy 2:8-10

_____

_____

Titus 2:11-14

_____

_____

_____

_____

2 Peter 1:3-9

_____

_____

_____

_____

1 Peter 4:7

_____

_____

_____

Acts 24:24-25

_____

_____

I found it particularly interesting that self-control came any where near an evangelistic message Paul presented to a political figure. In our culture today we spend most of our evangelistic message time on God's love (not that Paul didn't or that we shouldn't) and forgiveness. Self-control isn't usually on our docket for important points to address when holding up the light of truth for someone else to see the pathway to salvation. But it was part of the Gospel message at that moment Paul addressed Felix. Perhaps self-control was an important part of Paul's testimony. Perhaps it's an important part of ours, since in 1 Corinthians it is mentioned as the means through which Paul ensures that his ministry didn't derail and he become disqualified and unfruitful.

Read 2 Timothy 3:3-4 and note the usage of self-control:

_____

_____

_____

As the days grow to completion before the Lord returns, self-control, among many other facets of the fruit of the Spirit will be more counter-culture and therefore force our testimonies to show themselves more readily.

While the word "self-control" doesn't directly show up in these next verses, the concept is tied to them. Read and paraphrase these next verses and note the additional areas for us to practice exercising self-control:

Genesis 4:5-7

_____

_____

_____

_____

Psalm 101:3

_____

_____

Proverbs 4:23

_____

_____

Proverbs 12:27

_____

_____

_____

Romans 12:10-11

_____

_____

_____

_____

Ephesians 5:17-18

_____

_____

After the variety of contexts we've found self-control show up in the Bible, which ones surprised you?

_____

_____

_____

_____

Which areas are tugging at your heart for growth?

_____

_____

Self-control is an interesting concept. One that reaches into every facet of our life. It is also one that historically has been rather warped in the context of "holiness." In years past, asceticism (self-denial to the point of self-inflicted pain, torture, etc.) was considered mandatory for any measure of holiness. There's been cults using the name of Jesus who require sex practices/abstentions the Bible doesn't suggest, some of these groups have died out, some live on. I've known people who were convicted over a matter of self-control in their personal lives and proceeded to blanket everyone else around them with their same personal requirements for eating, sleeping, working, dress codes, family relationships, etc. When we do this we miss the essence of self-control. It's about us and God. It happens inside us and doesn't involve us controlling others, just our own messy little selves. There is freedom in Christ. And the pursuit of that freedom for the purpose of fruitfulness has been the heartbeat of this study. As we near our closing study, I am praying that no one would leave today's lesson with a view of self-control that isn't grounded in God's view of it. May self-control become one more glorious way God reveals His freedom in your life...freedom from old impulses, freedom from self-centeredness, freedom from self-indulgence and may He turn your life into a conduit for His power, truth and love to flow freely!

Spend some time writing out your 3x5 cards with verses from this week's study.

Day Five: The Enemy of Our Self-Control

As we close our time together, there's so many things on my heart and mind. I pray God's Word has been the loudest words in our journey. I pray that His words would be planted deeply in your heart and mine and that they would bear a harvest to our Father that is exceedingly, abundantly beyond all we could ask or imagine! I pray that our spiritual gardens would be freed from the enemy's stealing away of the abundance God desires for our life. And I pray that we would all bear fruit that lasts (John 15:16).

Now! To the topic of self-control!

Read and paraphrase the following verses, paying special attention to the connection between self-control and enemy influence:

1 Peter 5:8-9

_____

_____

_____

_____

Proverbs 25:28

_____

_____

1 Corinthians 7:3-5

_____

_____

The word for "sober-minded" in the NAS translation is often rendered "self-controlled."

To my married sisters, join me for a slight rabbit-trail. In Titus 2 we see our study word "self-control" pop up (NAS renders it "sober-minded" and it is a different word in the Greek from the fruit of the Spirit passage, but the concepts are tied). The older women are to teach the younger women to be a bunch of good stuff along with self-control. Now, one of the other concepts for passing-down from one generation of God-following women to the next is to be a "keeper" of the home. That word there is a compound word in the Greek. Part of the compound is "guard"[1] and was used of military guards who sat on top of a wall watching for enemies who might attack the city. A wise wife will guard her marriage by not depriving her husband (or herself) of the joy of intimacy God designed to be a blessing and protection to your marriage (1 Corinthians 7:3-5). The Proverbs 31 woman is also described as looking (or watching) well to the ways of her household. One of the best blessings you can give your children and grandchildren is the picture of a marriage the way (or as close to the way) God intended it--full of self-sacrificing love, but also being *in* love with one another, passionately, deeply and faithfully. When God instituted marriage, He said that His image was reflected in men and women as a joined pair. Our Father is best reflected when our marriages are planted in His design. Let us be wise women who look for enemy ensnarement that could come through cooled passions in our marriage. OK, back to the general ways we all exercise self-control...

I remember a women's retreat themed "Women of Service" when I was in high school. The speaker shared that we were made for service and that our lives will serve one of two masters: God or Satan. I was much younger in my faith and thought, "C'mon now! That seems a little restrictive! I think we can serve ourselves too..." She went on to explain how poorly we handle being the master of our own ship and that the position of master is always unfulfillable by us alone. I had more life to live before I could understand the truth of what she was saying...more mistakes to make, more trial-and-error to experience. Control of our lives belongs in the good, loving hands of our Father God. Our natural way of thinking deceives us into believing we can control our own lives. Slowly the enemy creeps in when our self-absorption gets the best of us. And we are like a city with no walls for his thieving. He can't possess us once we belong to Christ, but he sure can try to rip off every blessing God intended for us. He thieves what was meant to thrive!

In our culture of instant gratification and entertainment clamor, the enemy doesn't have to work too hard to find his way in. We all want convenience and comfort, but it can cost us our self-control if that convenience/comfort is even slightly off the path of design God laid out for us.

While I want to be careful about this topic because of how much the New Testament speaks about not debating over it, just take a tiny moment to consider how we eat, for example. After WWII chemical companies had less work and realized the stuff used to kill soldiers might be useful to kill bugs. True story. It worked. Fast forward a little more than half a century and food production is owned and controlled more by chemical companies than individual farmers or even farming conglomerates. We're chugging down so much stuff that has been modified off God's design and all of it adds up to ease for us. Ease in our kitchen, ease in the fields and farms, ease in the grocery stores. Many of my health-passionate Christian friends believe it's all a scheme of Satan to make us sick and kill us. It might just be human greed and love for convenience, but it seems logical to me that the enemy would capitalize on it as much as possible.

Here's another everyday life scenario: TV. Life can be so complicated and, well, TV just is such an easy escape from complicated. There's a "real life" problem solved in 30 minutes or less. Who wouldn't want to retreat into a fairyland like that? Relationships can be hard to find, keep, work through--but there's lots of friends on TV! So after all the stresses of the day, we can melt into the couch in front of our "cheap" entertainment and just let our minds rest. Even our dog loves TV. We'll go visit Eric's grandparents with Toby in tow and while the four of us play games, that funny little dog will leave us to go hang out with another relative and watch TV! But TV, as most of us know, has a lot of junk on it and it can keep us up later than we should be, thus robbing us of the rest we need to face what's coming the next day. TV can put pictures in our heads that take years to get out. It can be an open window for the enemy to shout into our lives.

I'm not saying it's morally wrong to watch TV or eat fast food. Heaven's no! I'm just saying these are easy areas to get sloppy--and they're culturally common areas for us to lack self-control.

Our technology is addictive and they've actually designed it that way. Our attention spans, as a culture, are shrinking because we are so used to being entertained that when something isn't entertaining, we just lose interest. Self-control is about strength and mastery. Whatever places a drain (or potential drain) on God's strength and mastery in your life needs guarding and perhaps unplugging. Because the enemy is waiting to find the castle of your heart like a city without walls.

Years ago, the woman who discipled me made an off-hand remark that was cemented into my mind. Life was swirling around her with difficulty and sadness. Her father had been an alcoholic so she had never touched the stuff. But she said something very interesting about it. She said, "You know, I could have drank responsibly all my life until this moment. If I was a drinker, I'd just get lost in a bottle because I'd want to do anything to escape this pain." Sometimes we can masterfully manage a matter, but then hit a snag that changes everything. Is your heart, mind and life cleared of obvious "fire hazards"?

Spend some time praying God's protection and filling over your life.

_____

_____

_____

_____

_____

_____

_____

_____

_____

I pray God's strength and mastery to fill your life with lasting fruitfulness in every way, my sister. May He protect the fruit of His Spirit in your heart and give you depth of discernment over the weeds, pests and everything that could hinder His best for you.

"You did not choose Me but I chose you, and appointed you that you would go and bear fruit, and that your fruit would remain, so that whatever you ask of the Father in My name He may give to you." John 15:16-17

Thank you so much for joining me for this journey through the Fruit of the Spirit. I pray you enjoyed this study and mostly that you are abundantly fruitful in our Lord! I always love to hear from sisters, so feel free to keep in touch! With much love and many blessings, April

Motl Ministries
www.MotlMinistries.com
info@motlministries.com

Praying to receive Christ as your Savior

Do you want to know God? He is the Creator of the Universe, the King of Kings, All-Powerful, and Eternal. Yet, His power and position do not keep Him at a distance from you. He desires a relationship, a close, intimate relationship with you, His child. If you want to begin a relationship with God, start here:

-**Admit** that you have made mistakes in your life. And that you do not measure up to God's standard of holiness. (Romans 3:23, Romans 6:23)

-**Believe** that Jesus is God. And that He came to earth, lived a sinless life, died in place for mankind's misdeeds, rose again three days later and now offers you the same resurrection power and newness of spiritual life. (John 3:16, 1 Corinthians 15:3-4)

-**Confess** that you need Jesus' free gift of salvation. Tell someone else that you have accepted Christ as your Savior. (Romans 10:13, 1 John 1:9)

You should share your heart with your Father freely, just as if He were sitting across the table from you. But here's a place for you to start:

Dear Father in heaven,
I come to you in the name of Jesus. I understand that I have sinned against You and I am sorry for my sins and the life that I have lived; I need your forgiveness.

I believe that your only begotten Son Jesus Christ shed His precious blood on the cross at Calvary and died for my sins. I believe that He rose from the grave and now offers me forgiveness and new life free from the bondages of sin I've known. I am now willing to turn from my sin.

You said in Romans 10:9 that if we confess the Lord our God and believe in our hearts that God raised Jesus from the dead, we shall be saved.

Right now I confess Jesus as the Lord of my soul. With my heart, I believe that God raised Jesus from the dead. This very moment I proclaim Jesus Christ as my own personal Savior and according to His Word.

Thank you Jesus for your unlimited grace which has saved me from my sins. I thank you Jesus that your kindness leads me to repentance. Transform my life so that I may bring glory and honor to You alone.

Thank You Jesus for dying for me and giving me eternal life.
Amen.

That is the simple beginning of a relationship with God. Find someone to share your decision with. Get into a solid, Bible-believing church where you can grow, find fellowship and accountability. Read God's Word, His love letter to you. Pray everyday and dedicate your heart to searching after the Lord. It is the journey of a lifetime!

Who I Am In Christ

I am the salt of the earth. Matthew 5:13
I am the light of the world. Matt 5:14
I am a child of God. John 1:12
I am part of the true vine, a channel of Christ's life. John 15:1,5
I am Christ's friend. John 15:15
I am chosen and appointed by Christ to bear His fruit. John 15:16
I am a slave of righteousness. Romans 6:18
I am enslaved to God. Rom. 6:22
I am a son of God; God is spiritually my Father. Rom. 8:14, 15; Galatians 3:26, 4:26.
I am a joint heir with Christ, sharing His inheritance with Him. Rom 8:17
I am a temple-a dwelling place - of God. His Spirit and His life dwells in me.
1 Corinthians 12:27; Ephesians 5:30
I am a new creation. 2 Corinthians 5:17
I am reconciled to God and am a minister of reconciliation. 2 Corinthians 5:18, 19
I am a son of God and one in Christ. Galatians 3:26, 28
I am an heir of God since I am a son of God. Galatians 4:6,7
I am a saint. Eph. 1:1, 1 Cor. 1:2; Phil. 1:1; Col. 1:2.
I am God workmanship - His handiwork - born anew in Christ to do His work.
Ephesians 2:10
I am a fellow citizen with the rest of God's family. Eph. 2:19
I am a prisoner of Christ. Eph 3:1; 4:1
I am righteous and holy. Eph 4:24
I am a citizen of heaven, seated in heaven right now. Phil 3:20, Eph 2:6
I am hidden with Christ in God. Colossians 3:3
I am an expression of the life of Christ because He is my life. Col 3:4
I am chosen of God, holy and dearly loved. Col. 3:12; 1 Thessalonians 1:4
I am a son of light and not of sudden darkness. 1 Thess. 5:5
I am a holy partaker of a heavenly calling. Hebrew 3:1
I am a partaker of Christ; I share in His life. Heb 3:14
I am one of God's living stones, being built up in Christ as a spiritual house.
1 Peter 2:5
I am a chosen race, a royal priesthood, a holy nation, a people for God's own
possession. 1 Pet. 2:9, 10
I am a stranger to this world in which I temporarily live. 1 Pet 2:11
I am an enemy of the devil 1 Pet 5:8 I am a child of God and I will resemble Christ
when He returns. 1 John 5:18

Sources:

1. Biblesoft's New Exhaustive Strong's Numbers and Concordance with Expanded Greek-Hebrew Dictionary. Copyright © 1994, 2003, 2006 Biblesoft, Inc. and International Bible Translators, Inc.

2. Vine's Expository Dictionary of Biblical Words, Copyright © 1985, Thomas Nelson Publishers.

3. http://www.adaa.org/about-adaa/press-room/facts-statistics stat source for anxiety issues

4. Farrel, Pam. *10 Best Decisions a Woman Can Make.* Harvest House Publishers: Eugene Oregon. 1999.

5. Dobson, Dr. James. *Emotions: Can You Trust Them?* Regal Books: Ventura, CA 1980.

www.ingramcontent.com/pod-product-compliance
Lightning Source LLC
Chambersburg PA
CBHW081537040426
42447CB00014B/3400